DANCING WITH IDOLATRY

Are you bowing to a false god?

Hensworth W. C. Jonas

xulon
PRESS

" *D*ancing *With Idolatry* is a profound and challenging book that gives pertinent awareness to the practical and subliminal dangers of idolatry. It is a call to examine one's life against the biblical record to see if honor that is due to God is being misappropriated."
—**Pastor Keelan A. Atkinson,** *Senior Pastor,* **Word Fellowship Reformed Baptist Church, Greensboro, North Carolina**

"Hensworth Jonas has written about a timeless subject that imperils every human heart. It is the natural desire for our hearts to be mirrors into which we look and worship ourselves. Pastor Jonas shows how these mirrors of self must be broken by the truth and divinely replaced with hearts that are windows through which we seek and worship the one, true God through Jesus Christ."
—**Dr. Don Whitney,** *Senior Associate Dean & Associate Professor of Biblical Spirituality,* **Southern Baptist Theological Seminary, Louisville, Kentucky**

"The most prevalent sin in the world is also the most revolting and damnable in God's sight—namely, idolatry. Dr. Jonas' piercing call for reformation and the removal of idols comes not a moment too soon for a world filled with false gods. With all the punch and rhythm of a powerful preacher, *Dancing with Idolatry* will make you "Amen!" in

agreement, then soberly reflect on your own heart and devotion to God."
—Pastor Thabiti Anyabwile, *Senior Pastor,* **First Baptist Church, Grand Cayman, Cayman Islands**

"John Calvin refers to the human heart as an idol factory. In this book, Hensworth Jonas encourages us to take a close look at this dangerous reality as he calls believers to pull down the idols that already exist there and guard against the manufacture of any more."
—Dr. Tom Ascol, *Senior Pastor,* **Grace Baptist Church, Cape Coral, Florida &** *Executive Director,* **Founder's Ministries**

DEDICATION

To the wife of my youth, Vandah M. Jonas, and the fruit of our union, Joshua Michael Jonas and Stephanie Hope Jonas: your support and prayers for my ministry of the Word of God over the years is evidence of God's extravagant grace and mercy in my life.

And to Loetta Landers of Nowata, Oklahoma: thanks for your wise and loving counsel and generous acts of caring when I struggled with my calling to the ministry as a young college student. Your passion for the supremacy of Christ in all things is a constant source of encouragement to me.

TABLE OF CONTENTS

INTRODUCTION

This book exists, not merely because there is a rich and disturbing biblical record concerning this issue of idolatry to draw on, but also because of my personal experience in it. To my shame, I am guilty of this spiritual treason of idolatry. I have placed temporal matters ahead of my God, making such matters the primary object of my devotion, interest, time, and spending. Martin Luther wrote that "whatever your heart clings to and relies upon, that is your God; trust and faith of the heart alone make both God and idol."[1]

Thank God, I found grace in His eyes. He gently exposed me, chastised me and gave me a hatred for my sin. I am now compelled to be committed and disciplined with the task, by His grace and power, of keeping myself unspotted by the world as well as the task of alerting my fellowmen about this poison. While I am grateful and confident in the fundamental change that has come over me, I have been occasionally discouraged by my subsequent and brief excursions in idolatry. But I am, however, also encouraged by the biblical remedies for this (1 John 1:9) and that by God's promise He is preserving me even as I persevere (Philippians 1:6).

I see idolatry on a daily basis. One of the clearest examples is in my evangelistic efforts as a pastor when I see men and women go to great pains and lengths to explain their personally invented concepts of the divine. They are usually very confident that their god will not do or say some of the things that a biblical and theologically Reformed presentation of the Gospel would affirm: issues such as the wrath of God, the exclusivity of Christ or the necessity of repentance. They are usually very shocked to hear me characterize their statements as a breach of the first and second commandments (Exodus 20:3-5). They are surprised when they are charged with creating a god that is a figment of their own imagination, a god whose attributes are fully under their control (and can be amended at any time), and one that is basically a celebration of their lusts.

I am afraid that many have dismissed all charges of idolatry because they have inaccurately and unbiblically defined it. I agree with Tim Keller's analysis of this matter:

> Sin isn't only doing bad things; it is more fundamentally making good things into ultimate things. Sin is building your life and meaning on anything, even a very good thing, more than on God. Whatever we build our life on will drive us and enslave us. Sin is primarily idolatry.[2]

These words bite and sting. They are compelling and piercing. These words basically put every man on a collision course with his idolatrous record. Have we bowed to false gods, putting ourselves in spiritual danger, even while we have been careless in not naming them as such? Are we playing little semantic games, spinning the truth concerning our real allegiance, even while we are at the same time gambling with our eternal destiny?

The reality before us is that the God of the Holy Bible does not change (Hebrews 13:8). The record of His response to idolatry, some of which we will explore in this book, is far too serious for anyone to ignore (Deuteronomy 32:16-22). It should drive all of us to our knees.

The sad reality about this spiritual treason of idolatry is not just how pervasive it is, but also how easy it is to commit. John Piper has helped us to understand how easy it is for us to be swallowed up in idolatry when he explained that "sin is what you do when you are not fully satisfied in God."[3] It is our dissatisfaction with God that drives our interest in alternatives to God. This is the prelude to our idolatry. We even make gods out of our opinions and analyses of the matter. It is so easy for us to imagine that our finite minds are ultimate and then to attempt to proudly run our lives as if we really know what we are talking or thinking about. We are clearly pretentious and have forgotten Proverbs 3:5-6.

It is my prayer that this brief look at the subject will encourage further study as well as bring repentance and conformity to the image of Christ.

I am very grateful for the assistance of Pamela Browman, one of my faithful staff members, for proof-reading my manuscript. Special thanks is also due to the Eldership and Diaconate of the Baptist Circuit of Churches—ECBM in Antigua & Barbuda and Dr. Tom Ascol of Cape Coral, Florida, for their advice and encouragement.

Hensworth W. C. Jonas
St. John's
Antigua & Barbuda
March, 2009

CHAPTER 1

THE TEMPTATION OF THE DANCE

My mouth was wide open for most of the trip. I couldn't believe my eyes. I had not seen anything like this on my native island of Antigua in the eastern Caribbean. At first, I looked at my guide over my spectacles trying to figure out whether he was putting me on or whether he was being serious. But he was very serious as he pointed out the monkey and other animal statues and shrines in yards of the homes in every village that we went through. I was on the island of Trinidad in the southern Caribbean and my guide was a fellow pastor. Those shrines and altars were Hindu gods, and yes, the seemingly normal, educated, professional people, with whom one did business in town, would go home at night to bow down before these monkey statues and family shrines. I know that this sounds like something from the primitive past, but it is very real and true today right here in the Caribbean.

To top it all off, I was told that I hadn't seen anything yet. My guide took me to a chapel where he showed me an idol that was supposedly worshipped by persons of all religious backgrounds on the island. They called it the Divine

Pastress. But what was it? It was a black doll dressed up in a wedding dress with a lot of gold and flowers all around it. Worshippers would enter at the side entrance of the chapel, kneel before this idol, which would supposedly accept no offerings but gold, which the worshippers freely presented in all forms of jewelry. I saw this with my own eyes. This idol was supposed to bring healing to all those with an acceptable offering. My guide speculated that this was probably one of the most lucrative money making scams in the nation of Trinidad & Tobago. Idolatry is still very much alive and well all over the world.

Many people would listen to this story and distance themselves from such activities. They would insist that such idolatry is not a part of their lives in any way. But is this the truth? There are, in fact, many idol worshippers today. Some may be of the primitive kind we have just described, while others are a little more sophisticated. Some may be nominally associated with some denomination of the Christian church, swearing allegiance to the immortal, invisible, only wise, true, and living God of the Holy Scriptures, but their true devotion and allegiance is to a cheap, temporal substitute. The human mind can be very creative in deifying that which it values the most. We can make idols out of anything, and this makes us no better than those who worship the traditional gods of the animistic and other heathen religions. We have made gods out of certain ideas, achievements, past times, entertainment, possessions, personalities, and even our own selves. These things are then worshipped as they become the supreme objects of our devotion, attention, spending, conversation, and social relationships. We can be as creative with our worship as we are with our idols.

ISRAEL AND IDOLATRY

The nation of Israel had begun a puzzling dance with idolatry in the time of Moses. In Exodus 32, Moses was on a unique mission on Mount Sinai. God had called him away from the people to give to him a clear statement of His law as well as other statutes for the government of the worship and civil life of the covenant people who were now a nation en route to the Promised Land. This law also included principles of morality for all mankind. These covenant people were the same people that God had just miraculously delivered from bondage in Egypt. These were the same people who, on coming out of Egypt, sang the praises of Jehovah and His servant Moses in their celebration of this amazing victory over tyranny and paganism. They knew that God was on their side for their deliverance was truly unmerited. Such slavery and bondage was common throughout the ancient world. It was obvious that their deliverance was a purposeful intervention of Sovereign Providence.

But the obvious became blurred by sin, the sin of idolatry. This is because it is far easier to take a man out of filth than it is to take the filth out of a man. Israel was out of the bondage of Egypt, but the bondage of Egypt was still in Israel. They were no longer living in physical bondage, but spiritual bondage was living in them. Their memories of Egypt were still vivid in their minds. Egypt was a pagan land of many idols, one of which was called Ptah, a god represented with the image of a calf or bull. But Egypt was also a prosperous land. Their material prosperity hardened the Egyptians in their spiritual darkness. The Egyptians gave all the credit for their material success to their heathen deities. The Hebrew slaves in Egypt had envied the wealth, status, and power of their oppressors. Many obviously came to believe that perhaps there was some merit and truth to the religion of Egypt. After all, some must have thought, just look at the results. It is indeed a dangerous thing to envy people who have much of this world's goods, especially when one does not know where they got it or where it will get them.

Israel fell into spiritual whoredom, dropping that which was real to chase an elusive, idolatrous dream. Exodus 32:1-8 tells the story of their dance with idolatry. How could the nation that was supposed to be the light of God to the nations of the world fall into such darkness? The children of Israel gave up the worship of the Almighty God, who is the source of all things, to embrace an idol in order to enjoy what seemed to be the prosperity of idolatry. It is important to note that elsewhere God characterized such apostasy as whoredom (Exodus 34:15). This speaks of how repulsive idolatry is in the sight of God. It is nothing less than a violation of one's sacred vows, stripping oneself of all dignity, making oneself a commodity to be used and discarded. How could they have come so far? How could they forget, so soon, the faithfulness of the true and living God? Have many of us done the same thing today? Is there anything in our lives that is more important than God? Have we bowed to a false god?

This is only one of the many incriminating stories of Israel's dance with idolatry, a phenomenon that appeared time and time again throughout her troubled history. This experience of the nation of Israel in the wilderness can enlighten us concerning certain characteristics or marks of idolatry. It will do us well to pay close attention to them that we may avoid them.

THE DANCE OF IMPATIENT HEARTS

Exodus 32:1 explains that Israel became tired of waiting for Moses to return from Mount Sinai. They were restless with impatience. Impatient hearts are wide open to idolatry. This young nation of Israel was not prepared to wait for anything or anyone. The brief delay in the return of God's servant was grabbed as an opportunity to abandon their Savior and Deliverer. This nation's impetuosity and shallowness made it refuse to submit to the agenda of the Lord God Almighty. The people were determined to do their own thing. How easily do those who have not been immunized with a dose of godly patience and contentment catch the virus of idolatry.

The enemy of our souls often uses our desire for the immediate to cloud our vision of the eternal. This immature insistence upon a 'now' response to everything has caused many a man and woman to turn their backs on God. It is clear for all to see that our generation has no use for a God who will not bless them with this world's goods immediately. In their eyes, God must play Santa Claus at their every whim to prove that He is real. This is somewhat similar to what J. B. Phillips described in his book, *Your God is Too Small*, in which ideas of God range from a personality that looks for opportunities to arrest persons who err or stray to one that is overly indulgent and would never want to detract from our hedonistic pursuits to one who is an "oblong blur" or whatever we want him to be.[2]

Our materialistic generation seems to evaluate everything according to the message and promises of a contrived right to prosperity and it wants it all right now. What our parents took two or three decades to achieve with hard work and perseverance, this generation desires to acquire in two or three months in a windfall. This is why so many are buried in debt and are at the mercy of the creditors. This is why so many are stressed out in the 'rat race' to maintain a lifestyle that is beyond their means. This is why so many have so much and enjoy it so little. This generation desires pleasure without principle because it must have it all now. With the same desire for immediate gratification it demands entertainment without edification, religion without repentance, prosperity without productivity, sexual involvement without spiritual intimacy and results without righteousness.

Have you bowed to a false god out of an unwillingness to wait on the providence of the Lord God Almighty or your unwillingness to look beyond the immediate for fulfillment?

We need the wisdom of the Ancient of Days to guide us, for He alone has the panoramic view of our lives: past, present, and future (Isaiah 46:10). Our limited, finite perspective on the issues and events of our lives will only confuse us and confound us even more. It is far better for us to place our lives in the mighty hands of sovereign Omnipotence, Omniscience, and Omnipresence. Why bow to the inanimate or the temporal when you can call upon El Shaddai, the Lord God Almighty?

THE DANCE OF IRRESPONSIBLE LEADERSHIP

Irresponsible spiritual leadership encourages idolatry. Of all people it was Aaron, Moses' brother and the priest of the Lord, who coordinated the design and production of the idol (Exodus 32:2-3). It is a dangerous thing to follow a spiritual leader who always gives you what you want, even when he knows that it will destroy you. The people wanted a replica of the Egyptian idol, so Aaron gave them what they wanted. Genuine spiritual leaders are more concerned about their people's spiritual health than their people's immediate happiness. Unhappiness is not a serious problem for it is easily solved with more information about the promises and providence of God concerning His people. Spiritual unhealthiness is a far more serious problem to solve for this requires a radical change in a person's entire being: mind, affections, and will.

When the people of God are assembled at any time, they should not attempt to function as a democracy. Throughout the Holy Scriptures it is clear that God has designed that they should be governed through a theocracy. God rules the congregation of His people through His Word, the Holy Scriptures (2 Timothy 3:16-17), which is to be proclaimed and applied by the spiritual leaders that He ordains (2 Timothy 4:2). The responsibility of the saints is to follow the spiritual leader as long as he rules by rightly dividing the

Word of God (Hebrews 13:17). Unfortunately, our generation has far too many Aarons, and too few Moses', to lead
them. As a result, many people are prone to fall into all
forms of idolatry. It is a situation where the tail is wagging
the dog or the cart is pulling the horse. What a monstrosity!
This only works in the cartoons. Thus, the people end up
leading according to the demands of their sinful desires, and
the leaders, like ignorant fools, end up following the whims
of a fickle and lustful people in order that their positions of
leadership may be maintained while the people are appeased
and quieted in a false security.

Biblical churches and Christians should pray that God
give them spiritual leaders who will feed their need and
not their greed, leaders who will work for God's approval
and not for man's applause and leaders who will promote
the eternal and not the temporal. It takes a strong leader to
magnify the power of God and not the pride of man, saying
'no' to idolatry and 'yes' to the Holy One of Israel.

THE DANCE OF CORRUPT THEOLOGY

Irrational and unscriptural beliefs are the foundation of
idolatry. Aaron not only fashioned the idol for Israel, he went
on to attribute the work of the God of Abraham, Isaac and
Jacob to the idol he had just crafted and instituted a feast in
honor of the idol (Exodus 32:4-5). Every evil act begins with
an evil idea or principle. Israel could not sink any lower in
corruption and blasphemy when the sovereign work of the
Lord God Almighty was attributed to an inanimate object.
And if that wasn't bad enough, the adoration and praise that
is due only to the Almighty was given to a creation of their
corrupt imagination. How could Aaron have used Jehovah's
name in connection with this idol?

In this act, Aaron and Israel walked all over the first
three of the Ten Commandments that condemn polytheism,
idolatry and blasphemy. They had irrational and unscriptural

views concerning creation, redemption, and providence. It is inevitable that the man who does not have a biblical answer concerning his origin, salvation, and preservation will prove that he is an idolater. It must be abundantly clear in your mind exactly who made you, who saves you, and who keeps you. A fallacious theology is bound to give birth to vain worship and futile service. Such ignorance and fallacy are never caused by the absence of divine revelation; they are rooted in the depravity and bondage of man's will based on his corrupt inheritance from Adam (Romans 1:18-25). Until Israel, by the grace of God, could break loose from this idolatrous Egyptian mentality, they would never understand that the finite could never displace the infinite and that impotence should never be worshipped in the place of Omnipotence.

Every biblical Christian can look back at his or her life of sinful rebellion prior to conversion and see that it was nothing but idolatrous Egyptian slavery. No one will make it to the Promised Land with an idolatrous Egyptian mentality. Heaven is for those who have been set free from such bondage. Your mind must be renewed.

Some churches do not like to get into doctrine and theology, because they are afraid that it will cause contention and quarrels. But what you believe to be true makes all the difference in the world. Your mind must be focused on the Promised Land, for repentance demands that idolatrous Egypt be a thing of the past. We all know of the horrors of idolatrous Egypt, of the sinful life. We have all been there and, unfortunately, many more are still there. But, thank God, we do not have to stay there for our Savior and Deliverer has come. This is the hope of true believers in Christ Jesus. In idolatrous Egypt the believer was a slave to sin, but now, having been redeemed, he can freely march to Zion, the beautiful city of God. In idolatrous Egypt, the believer had no inheritance but a future of hopelessness and sorrow, as he labored under the whip of the enemy, but now in Christ he has a title deed in the realms of Glory. In idolatrous Egypt no one cared about just another slave's name, but now the believer's name is written in the Lamb's Book of Life. In idolatrous Egypt the believer was buried in despair, but now, by the grace of God, he has nothing to fear. The saints of God have been saved from the condemnation and penalty of the idolatrous Egyptian mentality; they are being saved from the control or power of this mentality; and, one day, they will be saved from the very company or presence of this mentality.

THE DANCE OF IMMORAL CONDUCT

A proliferation of immorality is the sure companion of idolatry. Where idols are worshipped, people let themselves go. Anything goes. There isn't even a sense of shame. They drown their shame in licentious behavior and are only able to bear it with the aid of all kinds of chemical and emotional intoxication. In Exodus 32:6, the children of Israel, in the presence of their idol, had their own version of the contemporary New Orleans Mardi Gras or the national carnivals of the Caribbean islands and Brazil. In this verse, the words 'rose up to play' refer to the worship of the bull-god, which inspires lewd, sensual dances that formed a part of the worship in the fertility cults of that day.[3] These dances were the means of stirring up sexual desire to the point that the whole assembly of the people would be quickly immersed in a frenzy of a filthy, carefree, sexual orgy. In this frenzy the people did anything with their bodies with anyone they could find. Is this what the chosen nation of God had come to? Are these the same people that the Lord gloriously rescued from Egypt? O what a shameful abomination! What a disgraceful mockery of the holy name of God. But this is the reality: wherever there is idolatry there will also be perversion and immorality, and wherever there is perversion and immorality there will also be idolatry. They are inextricably linked.

If we are honest about our experiences in sin, we will all admit that our darkest moments of immorality were related to the idolization of someone or something in our lives. Sexual immorality comes with the lustful focusing upon and idolization of someone to whom one is not biblically and legally married. Extortion, embezzlement, and all forms of theft often come with the idolization of a lifestyle that one cannot afford. Violence, bitterness, hate, and murder come with the idolization of a grudge until it grows into a vendetta. Perjury and all falsehood come with the idolization of one's temporal security, forgetting one's eternal security. Envy and covetousness come with the idolization of competition and greed at the expense of contentment. Disrespect and insubordination comes with the idolization of one's pride, displacing the divine order of things. The profaning of one's day of worship comes with the idolization of personal pleasure and convenience, displacing the worship of God. Immorality is always present and growing wherever there is idolatry.

ABORTING THE DANCE

It is obvious that the dance with idolatry is dangerous. It must be ended. But it often seems to be a difficult thing to just walk away, for in this dance, even if you let go of your partner, your partner may still be holding on to you. What can you do if you really want to leave the dance floor of filth with such a partner holding on to you? Is there a courteous way to abandon what is clearly inappropriate and unhelpful? Should you even care about how or why you leave the floor? There are some helpful principles for those who are serious about making a break with their idols and making the real God their priority.

First, there will be no break with idolatry where there isn't authentic saving faith in and intimacy with the Lord Jesus Christ (1 John 5:18-21, 1 Corinthians 10:21). It is in coming into a vital relationship with Christ, trusting only in

His atoning sacrifice on Calvary, that the chains of false religion and superstition are broken. Tom Steller's comments on 1 John 5:18-21 are very useful in establishing the notion that truly experiencing Christ is the solution to the problem of establishing the reality of God or answering the temptation to create God-substitutes.

> The key word, of course, is "true." True in the sense of "real." The purpose of Jesus coming into the world according to verse 20 was to help us understand that God is real, that he really does exist, he really is light, he really is love. God is not a figment of our imagination. He is the ultimate reality of the world....What is the solution to this doubt? The apostle John's response is "Jesus." Jesus is the evidence that God is real. According to verse 20 Jesus, the Son of God, "came and has given us understanding in order that we might know him who is true." In 4:7, 10 we are told that God, by sending Jesus to die for our sins, manifested his love for us, that is, he made his love real, concrete, tangible, unmistakable for those who had eyes to see. The realness of Jesus guarantees for us the realness of God. That's why John is so concerned throughout this letter that his readers remain true to the real Jesus.[4]

Second, let everything about your life become an expression of your worship and service to Christ (Romans 12:1-2, Matthew 6:33). The saints of God should never have a life that is compartmentalized. We do not have a religious life and a secular life. We are to live a Christian life in all areas of life. Whether the context is the meetings of the church or the busyness and business of the marketplace, our Lord and our faith must be with us all the time. Do not magnify anything in your life above Christ. Christ should not merely be a part of your life. Christ must be your life. Let Christ be the reason why you do anything that you do. This will reserve all devotion to Christ alone. If you are taking a walk, walk to the glory of Christ. If you are taking a trip, travel to the praise of Christ. If you are doing any assignment, work to the honor of Christ. If you open your mouth to talk, exalt the name of Christ in whatever you say, and let it be edifying to all who hear it. Saturate your life with the love of Christ. If someone cuts you, bleed the love of Christ. You will never bow to an idol if the Lord Jesus Christ is magnified in every aspect of your life.

Third, kill the habits of idolatry with a radical separation from every appearance of the yoke of bondage (2 Corinthians 6:14-18). Idolatry is a thing that must not be abandoned gradually. You must attack it with urgency. You must burn your bridges behind you. All the paraphernalia of your idol must be destroyed immediately. Leave nothing around you that reminds you of your former bondage. Satan has used many people and experiences to trap us in our past sins. Do not let him rub your past failure in your face. If it is an old photograph that he uses to discourage you, tear it up and burn it. If it is a gift that was used in your seduction, throw it in the trash. You should not even care about its commercial value for nothing on earth is worth more than your soul (Mark 8:36-37). If it is an old friend that Satan uses to wear you down time and time again, break off the friendship now! Do not let them prove your profession of faith to be false and drag you into hell. It is written in 1 John 2:15, "Do not love the world or the things in the world. If anyone loves the world, the love of the Father is not in him." The idols of our past must never become monuments for us to look at. They must be broken down immediately. It is only when we break down the idols of empty religion that God may build in us religion that is pure and undefiled. We need to break down the idols of hedonism, all pleasure at the expense of righteousness, that God may build in us a joy unspeakable and fill of glory.

The idols of bitterness and hatred must be destroyed that God may build in us a perfect love which casts out all fear. We must forsake the idols of ungodly sex that God may build in us a heart that craves purity and real intimacy. We must treat with contempt the idols of ill-gotten gain that God may build in us a commitment to fair play and decency. We must break down the idols of dishonesty that God may build in us a clear conscience and a peace that passes all understanding. We must destroy the idols of greed that God may build in us a heart of contentment. Break down every idol in your life, for the Lord God Almighty is a jealous God (Exodus 34:14). His is a holy jealousy. Every creature should bow before the Creator alone. Have you bowed to a false god?

If you have a right relationship with God and have experienced the confidence of being in the will of God, like Shadrach, Meshach, and Abednego you would prefer to be burned in a furnace than to bow to a false god (Daniel 3:16-18). You will announce your allegiance to the true and living God and like, the apostle Peter, affirm your faith with the words, "Lord, You are the Christ, the Son of the Living God" (Matthew 16:16). End the dance with idolatry, and heed the invitation from the psalmist, "Oh come, let us worship and bow down; Let us kneel before the Lord our Maker" (Psalm 95:6).

CHAPTER 2

THE DISPLACEMENT OF GOD

You should have very little difficulty in affirming that everyone, at some time or another, must have someone, something, or some idea upon which to focus his or her attention, adoration, passion and commitment. This is the very nature of what we call life and living. We all live for something or someone, whether we want to admit it or not. Furthermore, it is not very difficult for us to discover what the object of our devotion is. Should someone threaten to remove it or should we suddenly lose it (even temporarily), our dispositions and actions would manifest our brokenness and loss of reason to live. This is at the heart of the problem of suicide, for people think of taking their lives, not because they really want to die, but when they can see nothing for which to live. This is also the heart of the problem of chemical abuse and other kinds of so-called codependent behavior, for people only think of using these temporary escapes from reality when they can find nothing that makes life worthwhile.

We must ask the question: Is the Lord truly our God? With this question I am simply asking you to honestly admit to yourself that there might be something in your life or someone that is more important to you than the God of the Holy Scriptures. Because of this thing or person in your life, any talk of the God of Abraham, Isaac and Jacob must take the back seat. Richard Gaffin puts it like this:

> Because we are, each of us, the image of God, we will worship, in fact we must worship someone or something, either our original, as we should, or, with the illusion that we are the original or our own ultimate point of reference, ourselves. If the latter, we will give ourselves over, with the full, still efficient resources of our imaging capacities, to some figment, some distorted image, focused on ourselves or on some aspect of the world, ultimately seen as an extension of ourselves. What Calvin observed long ago is no less true today: the human heart, our image-bearing and image-fashioning nature, is an idol factory.[1]

Idols are simply monuments to what we value most in life. For instance, if you value illicit sex more than anything else, you will idolize the filthy movies on television or in the theatre, the pornography, as well as your friends and partners who will encourage you in your promiscuity and fornication. This will be your preoccupation, your focus of devotion. If the pride of feeling superior to others is the most important thing to you, you will idolize the car, house, money, pretty face, clothes, academic credentials, and other 'possessions' that make it easier for you to look down on others and exalt yourself.

We have deliberately used the words 'idol' and 'god' to speak of the object or objects of our devotion. This is a rather blunt way to make the point, for it rudely awakens us to the idolatry in our lives. We must state this frankly even though many will continue to resist the notion that they are in fact idol worshippers. If you are numbered among such persons, it is only natural that you would find it offensive that someone would insult your modern sensibilities and intellect and associate you with primitive paganism. If you are wondering if I have mistakenly overstated this analysis, I must make it abundantly clear that any biblical treatment of idolatry must affirm that anything or anyone that gets more of your attention than God, or any idea that you embrace that distorts the biblical revelation concerning the person of God, makes you an idolater. Martin Luther wrote:

> To whatever we look for any good thing and for refuge in every need, that is what is meant by 'god.' To have a god is nothing else than to trust and believe in him from the heart...To whatever you give your heart and entrust your being, that, I say, is really your god.[2]

You may be a modern secular or religious pagan, but you are just like the primitive pagans. It is a very safe conclusion that the world has not improved spiritually and morally since the ancient days. We have technological advances that have made us more efficient with our sinful schemes. As a matter of fact, the world has gotten worse. The world is more pagan than it ever has been. You may want to call what we see today a sophisticated or even intellectual paganism, but a pagan is a pagan before the sovereign and jealous God of the Holy Scriptures. Your consuming passion or whatever your number one interest is amounts to the same thing to God as if you constructed a statue out of wood or metal and bowed down before it. If Matthew 6:33 is not being obeyed in your life, you are deep in the whoredom of idol worship, you are prostituting yourself before the face of God for God and God alone is the legitimate object of your worship.

BOW TO THE CREATOR—NOT THE CREATION

The prophet Isaiah faced the problem of idolatry in his day and launched an attack on it in Isaiah 46:5-13. The general theme of this prophecy was the deliverance of Israel through the destruction of Babylon. The prophet proclaims the Lord's words in the first person, giving us a taste of the raw and overwhelming authority of the voice of the Lord. What does He say to us? Isaiah 46:5-7 reads:

> To whom will you liken Me, and make Me equal and compare Me, that we should be alike? They lavish gold out of the bag, and weigh silver on the scales; they hire a goldsmith, and he makes it a god; they prostrate themselves, yes, they worship. They bear it on the shoulder, they carry it and set it in its place, and it stands; from its place it shall not move. Though one cries out to it, yet it cannot answer nor save him out of his trouble.

The point is simple. It is ridiculous to worship something that is created, whether directly from the hand of the Creator or from the raw materials shaped by a created being. It is a great insult to the Creator to give any aspect of His creation, inanimate or animate, the glory that is due to His name. But how many of us do this in our lives daily?

When you think about it, idolatry seems downright silly. But why, then, is it so appealing? The appeal may come from the fact that man remains in control when he creates his own idol, his own god. "They bear it on the shoulder, they carry it and set it in its place, and it stands..." (Verse 7a). This kind of god, this idol, will never question the morality and ethics of your behavior. This kind of god welcomes every kind of self-indulgence. Licentiousness is the rule of life when you create your own god. As we said before, with your own idol you can make up the rules and change them whenever you feel like it. You are in charge. J. I. Packer has clearly explained the idolater's position as opposed to the doctrine of the aseity of God.

> God's self-existence is a basic truth. At the outset of his presentation of the unknown God to the Athenian idolaters, Paul explained that this God, the world's Creator, "is not served by human hands, as if he needed anything, because he himself gives all men life and breath and everything else" (Acts 17:23-25). Sacrifices offered to idols, in today's tribal religions as in ancient Athens, are thought of as somehow keeping the god going, but the Creator needs no such support system. The word *aseity*, meaning that he has life in himself and draws his unending energy from himself…was coined by theologians to express this truth, which the Bible makes clear…[3]

This is exactly what the people who promote the idea of situation ethics are doing. For these people, there are no moral absolutes; everything is relative. So everyone does whatever he pleases, for his god (which he sometimes calls his conscience) does not bother him about it.

This is only appealing to the depraved mind, the mind that is yet in bondage in the darkness of sin. When a heart or mind is quickened by God, when a man is enabled by the grace of God to see the filth of his sinful life and his desperate state, having been brought out of darkness into God's marvelous light, he does not want a God that he can carry around; he wants a God that can carry him, for he realizes that left to himself he will get nowhere worth going. The prophet Isaiah makes the ability of all false gods abundantly clear: "…from its place it shall not move. Though one cries out to it, yet it cannot answer nor save him out of his trouble" (verse 7b). If you are responsible for carrying your god, when you need help, you can only depend on yourself, and you only have yourself to congratulate for your successes. This is at the heart of the contemporary cult of self-worship that is promoted in the media and secular academia with Abraham Maslow as one of its apostles.

Idolatry is often toyed with when one is not in a desperate situation. Its emptiness is quickly exposed when real trouble comes for it will be obvious that it cannot demonstrate its efficacy. When you are in trouble, you will be foolish to run to the idolatrous castles that are built in the sand. Like the psalmist you should say "From the end of the earth I will cry to You, when my heart is overwhelmed; lead me to the rock that is higher than I" (Psalm 61:2).

It is so easy for us to fill our bellies with the meat from the royal tables of Babylon prepared for the feasts of the idols. We should instead hold out for the sweet fruit of righteousness from the sacred table of the Lord. In times of trouble you want a God who will answer with tangible help when you call. When you are discouraged, you want a God whose rod and staff will comfort you. When you are insecure, you want a God who will not suffer your foot to be moved. When you feel vulnerable, you want a God who will hide you in His pavilion. You do not want anything or contraption that you can design or mold as your god. You want the God who made you. You do not want some fairy tale, pie in the sky figment of your imagination to call your god. You want the Rock of Ages. You want the Ancient of Days. So, will the real God please stand?

BELIEVE GOD'S REVELATION—NOT VAIN REASONING

Idolatry is rooted in a state of denial. It is based on denying the obvious concerning God's natural revelation (Psalm 19:1-6) as well as His special revelation (2 Timothy 3:16-17; Romans 1:18-23). One must be engaged in a rebellious, purposeful and deliberate effort to forget or revise the reality that one has experienced or been exposed to. The prophet Isaiah revealed the Lord's words on the matter:

> Remember this, and show yourselves men; recall to mind, O you transgressors. Remember the former things of old, for I am God, and there is no other; I am God, and there is none like Me, declaring the end from the beginning, and from ancient times things that are not yet done, saying, 'My counsel shall stand, and I will do all My pleasure,' calling a bird of prey from the east, the man who executes My counsel, from a far country. Indeed I have spoken it; I will also bring it to pass. I have purposed it; I will also do it (Isaiah 46: 8-11).

We all have a great deal of sympathy for the man whose ignorance is the result of some semblance of innocence. But we all despise the ignorance that comes from carelessness, irresponsibility, apathy, or rebellion. This is a willful ignorance. In such cases, one does not know because one does not want to know. This is often man's problem with the revelation of God. Our problem is usually not a lack of information about God and His will. The problem is usually that the knowledge of God is despised and suppressed in the heart. The apostle Paul wrote in Romans 1:20-21,

> For since the creation of the world His invisible attributes are clearly seen, being understood by the things that are made, even His eternal power and Godhead, so that they are without excuse, because, although they knew God, they did not glorify Him as God, nor were thankful, but became futile in their thoughts, and their foolish hearts were darkened.

The prophet Isaiah presents a call from God for all to remember who He has revealed Himself to be. There is a major point of distinction here. In the worship of the true God, worshippers are preoccupied with what their God has to say concerning Himself. They want the Word of God. They want a real man of God to say, "Thus says the Lord." On the other hand, in idol worship, the worshipper does all the talking because his idol, his god, has nothing to say and can say nothing. The reason why some people do not like to hear the preaching of the Word of God is that they are made to stop talking and listen. Preaching is probably the only method of instruction that actually humbles the listener. Most listeners would much rather have debates or discussions or dialogue because their idol, their god, allows them to do all the talking. But a unique fact about Jehovah God is that His true spokesmen will never be muzzled, for God will not allow it and the true worshippers will not tolerate it. You can know that your religion has become man-centered when the whole counsel of God is not received in preaching. You can know that your religion is man-centered when there is far more dancing than there is studying. When the sharing of your feelings and experiences take precedence over the declaration of the Word of God, you have created an idol of self.

But what has God said? What is he like? He is unique in the universe (verse 9). He has established, and will accomplish, His purpose (verse 10). He has all means at His disposal in carrying out His holy will (verse 11). What a mighty God is He! The prophet reminds us of the importance of remembering these things. We must remember the former things of old for the new ways have taught us nothing but selfishness and pride, and we run the risk of witnessing the ranks of true believers become contaminated with worldly wisdom. Forgetfulness is just too costly, for time is too short and hell is too long. The Lord must have the preeminence in all things.

BROKENNESS IS THE SOLUTION—NOT STUBBORNNESS

Ignoring the declarations of God has never lessened their severity. God's hatred of idolatry will remain unabated. As you continue to kick against pricks, you will certainly reap what you have sown. The Lord is never intimidated by the toothless bite of our arrogant defiance. Our stubbornness will never halt or retard the sure approach of His righteousness. Isaiah reveals the pointed words of the Lord to be:

Listen to Me, you stubborn-hearted, who are far from righteousness: I bring My righteousness near, it shall not be far off; my salvation shall not linger. And I will place salvation in Zion, for Israel My glory (Isaiah 46:12-13).

The presence of the idolatrous forces of evil and all wickedness of men has never kept the Lord from pouring out His wrath upon evil doers and pouring out His blessings upon the remnant He has reserved unto Himself. Come what may, there will be joy in Zion for the elect of God. So let the wicked man come with the venom of his hate, for he will never stop the rejoicing in Zion. Isaac Watts wrote in a hymn:

Let those refuse to sing
Who never knew our God,
But children of the heavenly King
May speak their joys abroad.

Let those with hearts of stone attack the walls of Zion, for Zion is bound to stand. Martin Luther wrote in a hymn, "A mighty fortress is our God, a bulwark never failing."

Even the wicked can be made to come to Zion's defense if God demands it or if He is pleased to reserve for them a heart of flesh. A lie is only threatening when the truth is concealed. But the truth brings the glowing light of freedom and salvation. The counsel of the ungodly, the way of sinners, and the seat of the scornful (Psalm 1:1) will only sow the seeds of iniquity as long as there is no salvation in Zion. But the Lord has said, "...my salvation shall not linger. And I will place salvation in Zion, for Israel My glory."

There is a call here for the true saints of God not to despair. Why? The Lord will place salvation in Zion. The road may be rough and the journey tough, but the elect of God are promised the victory. They have no 'bags to pack' for they are promised all they need in Zion. The image is clear that as they travel through the barren land, they must be satisfied with a tent. They should not get too attached to their present surroundings. They should thank God for what they have, but thank Him even more that what they have does not have them.

Do you have that broken and contrite heart? Does your displacement of God with temporal substitutes cause you to mourn? Or are you so puffed up with pride that you cannot even hear the Word? Are you so in love with your sin and married to your idols that you are indifferent to the Word of God? Remember: brokenness is the solution, not stubbornness.

FEEDING YOUR LUST AND GREED

Is the Lord truly your God? Are you sure that the object of your worship is the God of Abraham, Isaac and Jacob? It should grieve the heart of every true Christian that day by day the whoredom of idolatry proliferates. So many spend all of their time building monuments to the lust of their flesh, the lust of their eyes, and the pride of life (1 John 2:16). They work so hard at their idol building, that they have completely forgotten the former things of old. Idolatry has made some of us so busy making a living that there is no time to really live. Idols soon become monsters, for they are never satisfied. You will feed them forever for you will actually be feeding your own lusts and not true love; you will be feeding your greed and not your need.

The elect of God are admonished by Christ with the words, "...but lay up for yourselves treasures in heaven, where neither moth nor rust destroys and where thieves do not break in and steal" (Matthew 6:20). Have you displaced your God? John Calvin explains it like this:

> Mingled vanity and pride appear in this, that when miserable men do seek after God, instead of ascending higher than themselves as they ought to do, they measure him by their own carnal stupidity, and neglecting solid inquiry, fly off to indulge their curiosity in vain speculation. Hence, they do not conceive of him in the character in which he is manifested, but imagine him to be whatever their own rashness has devised. This abyss standing open, they cannot move one footstep without rushing headlong to destruction. With such an idea of God, nothing which they may attempt to offer in the way of worship or obedience can have any value in His sight, because it is not Him they worship, but, instead of Him, the dream and figment of their own heart.[4]

If you have made an idol out of anything or anyone, the call is to break it down right now. Please break it down for it is coming down anyway, for our God is a jealous God and His jealousy is holy. Break it down for if you let God break it down you might go down with it. The Lord Jesus Christ warned, "For what will it profit a man if he gains the whole world, and loses his own soul?" (Mark 8:36). We should break down the idols for this life is but a vapor (James 4:14) and we are better off setting our affections on things above and not on things on the earth (Colossians 3:2).

CHAPTER 3

THE DISLOYALTY OF IDOLATRY

We have all, in this generation, witnessed the devaluation of the principle of loyalty. Signing the dotted line does not amount to anything these days. Reneging on one's commitments now seems to be the rule, not the exception. People are making promises all the time and have no battle of conscience in abandoning them. The prevailing attitude around us is one that says, "I will stay if I'm enjoying myself." Hedonism, personal comfort, personal image, and filthy lucre have displaced values such as considering the needs of others, morality, the value of one's word, and Christian commitment in deciding questions about what one will be loyal to. Selfishness seems to have the ascendency. It is clearly a driving principle in idolatry. Some scholars have even claimed that selfishness is the core or root principle, the very basis, of all sin and iniquity.[1]

Most people seem to be always holding out for something better, even after committing themselves. They don't want to get too attached to anyone or anything for something better might come up at any moment. They don't want to work hard building anything for that is too long term and it takes commitment. They prefer to live in borrowed nests and sit on stolen eggs. They are rolling stones, gathering no moss. They will give a half-hearted involvement in a project, hoping to claim any available benefits, without getting in with both feet. Getting in with both feet would keep them from avoiding taking responsibility for any liabilities that might result.

Idolatry is the worst kind of disloyalty. It is even worse than treason and adultery for these things are usually a part of it or are the result of it. In idolatry, the immortal, invisible, only wise God is not only betrayed, but also dishonored. Here, the Creator of all things is being displaced by created things in a competition for the highest place of devotion in a person's life. This is the ultimate insult. God hates all sin, but there is no sin that He hates more than the sin of idolatry. God desires absolute and consistent loyalty from His children. Loyalty is an indispensable quality if one is to have an authentic relationship of righteousness with God.

UNFINISHED BUSINESS

In Deuteronomy 13, slavery in Egypt was now a thing of the past. There was no more fear of Pharaoh among the children of Israel. As a matter of fact, most of the people, at this point, did not even know what he looked like. A whole new generation had arisen on the journey from Egypt through the wilderness on the way to the Promised Land. Disobedience and murmuring had brought the judgment of the Lord upon their parents, denying them the privilege of seeing the new home that God had promised Israel. In the wilderness the whole nation had been fickle and consistently inconsistent. The question now was: would this new generation be any different? Would they learn from the folly of their parents? Was the legacy of faith transferred at all or did it die with those who died in the wilderness?

The privilege of entering the Promised Land also brought great responsibility to this second generation of Israel. God had given them the title deeds to the Promised Land in His covenant with Abraham (Genesis 12:1-3; Nehemiah 9:7-8), but He left them the task of clearing it before they could build on it. Thus, all the children of Israel stood in the plains of Moab, poised for the invasion of Canaan. The Canaanites were a wicked people who were under a judicial sentence by God with a 'ban' to wipe them from the face of the earth. The Lord could look upon their sin no longer. Thus, the Lord was about to fulfill a double purpose in the demise of these people. He would show both grace and justice in His action. By grace He gave Israel an inheritance while at the same time administering justice in ridding the earth of the wicked Canaanites. In this endeavor, the recipients of grace were charged with the responsibility of being the instruments of justice. Israel had to rise to the challenge of removing the wicked Canaanites from the face of the earth.

We should always welcome the Lord's invitation for us to participate in His gracious purposes in our lives. The God of Abraham, Isaac and Jacob does not encourage laziness. God had blessed them with manna in the wilderness from the heavens, but He still expected them to go out and gather it. God will bless us with fish for our nets, but He will still ask us to cast our nets out into the deep (Luke 5:4). God will bless us with a guarantee of victory in the battle of life, but He still demands that we put on the whole armor of God (Ephesians 6:10-11). God will bless us with both revelation and intelligence, but He still expects us to study. The apostle Paul admonished Timothy with the words, "Be diligent to present yourself approved to God, a worker who does not need to be ashamed, rightly dividing the word of truth" (2 Timothy 2:15). God had blessed Israel with the Promised Land, but they had to go in and possess it. Fatalism is false religion at its core. The Sovereign God of the universe who foreordains everything that comes to pass is also pleased to use means in the execution of His purposes. A religion is false if it has man doing either everything or nothing. True religion recognizes that it is God who ultimately does everything, and one of the things that He does is to give man something to do. The responsibility of man is one of the out workings of the sovereignty of God.

Was Israel faithful with this responsibility? No. They did not rid the land of all its wicked occupants. They thought that they could peacefully coexist with the enemies of God. They made alliances with the ungodly. They sought to negotiate on matters which God had settled, and were settled on matters which God instructed them to contend. From the onset, Israel sowed the seeds of her ultimate apostasy. But God, with His great faithfulness to His covenant, permitted them some semblance of nationhood in the land despite the fact that the occupation was incomplete. God's grace and mercy are truly amazing.

It was now time for maintenance. This is where we prove what we are really made of. Of course, anybody can get something started. The real test is about who can endure. Was Israel going to abandon the call of God to maintain its national purity and call to holiness? They had already compromised in the invasion of the land by not ridding it entirely of its occupants. How far would they go? Would the children of Israel remain loyal to God in the midst of the corruption around them with all the enticing sensuality? This is why the book of Deuteronomy was written. It was not a second law (as its name seems to suggest), but a second presentation of the law, specifically designed for this second generation of Israel that knew not the bondage of Egypt. What instructions were they given in order that they might be shielded from idolatry? What can we learn from the admonition given to Israel that would help us to maintain our loyalty to God in this generation?

LOYALTY TESTED BY IMPRESSIVE PERSONALITIES

Israel was given some strict instructions concerning the vetting of the credentials and credibility of anyone who claimed to possess the prophetic gift from God (Deuteronomy 13:1-5). The impressive signs and wonders presented by would-be prophetic persons who also pointed the people to the veneration of strange deities were to be rejected. Falling for such spectacles exposes one's true love and loyalty. This is how one fails the test sent by God. False prophecy was a capital offence in Israel for it dishonored the true and living God who was Israel's deliverer. Foolish idolaters are often fooled by someone. Israel was warned that charismatic, flamboyant and impressive spiritual leaders can be a source of error and spiritual disaster.

True believers are to guard their minds and screen the doctrine that they receive. These verses are like a page out of today's newspaper. There are so many people claiming divine revelation, supernatural abilities and prophetic insight. Many of them are able, by demonic power, to impress you with seemingly credible verification of their abilities (Deuteronomy 13:1-2). This is not unlike what we are told concerning the 'man of sin' in 2 Thessalonians 2:1-12. Many false prophets will have very compelling stories and teachings that are nothing but sugarcoated lies. The true believer must think clearly.

The great test of the truthfulness of the one who claims the prophetic gift is whether or not he or she departs from any aspect of the Word of God or attempts to entice listeners away from their allegiance to God. Deuteronomy 13:3 tells us that God allows these false messengers to do their work that He may test or expose the loyalty of His elect. How gullible are you? What is your price? What does it take for you to sell out your faith for the most popular idol? What will it take to make you leave your covenant commitments like others have done? Every doctrine or messenger that does not encourage exclusive obedience to God is not of God. Such persons should not be supported, but rejected (Deuteronomy 13:5). The seriousness and intensity of this rejection is seen in the fact that such false prophecy was to be a capital offense in Israel. The motive of such a false prophet is to steal the glory and honor that belongs only to the Lord God Almighty.

It is imperative that we learn to stay focused in a crooked and perverse world. We must learn to mind our business, which should be the Lord's business. Make no mistake about this fact. If you are hungry for the latest trends you will certainly be taken for a ride off the deep end. If you must have new ideas about spirituality, the old time-tested religion will never be good enough for you. If you must experience sensational thrills, you will never be satisfied with the disciplined study of the Word of God. If you are hungry for carnal excitement, you will never know the peace of God which passes all understanding. But the Holy Scriptures say: "Blessed are those who hunger and thirst for righteousness, for they shall be filled" (Matthew 5:6). With what are they to be filled? The answer is "love, joy, peace, longsuffering, kindness, goodness, faithfulness, 23 gentleness, self-control. Against such there is no law" (Galatians 5:22-23).

We live in a generation that demands that everything be entertaining, whether it be work, study, or church. Everything is evaluated through the microscope of hedonism. Truth is subjected not to logically presented inspired revelation, but to the spectacle and manipulation of signs and wonders. Thus, the idea with the greatest sideshow wins. Biblical authority is thrown out the door. Of course, Satan, the great counterfeiter, is fully capable of producing lying signs and wonders (2 Thessalonians 2:9). True believers need to guard their mind and screen the doctrine that they receive.

LOYALTY TESTED BY FAMILY CONNECTIONS

The Hebrew people were challenged to not let even close family ties entice them into idolatry (Deuteronomy 13:6-11). They were to expose such idolatrous family members and take a prominent role in the application of capital punishment upon the same to keep the people of God free from the curse of this sin.

True believers are to guard their affections and screen the relationships that they embrace. This is one of the most difficult teachings in the Holy Scriptures. It is one of the greatest tests of loyalty. It is here that many people prove whether or not Christ is Lord of their lives. Will you allow your family and loved ones to pull you away from Christ? The admonition here is that there should be no intimate fellowship with relatives and friends who encourage ungodliness and idolatry. We are taught here that not only are we to reject their counsel, we are to take the lead in opposing them in the assembly of the saints. The text tells us of the power of such a stance, for others will fear (verse 11) when they realize that the only standard among the people of God is holiness unto the Lord. The idea that "blood is thicker than water" — a common saying in the Caribbean — is totally unbiblical, especially when righteousness is the water. The only blood that matters to God is the blood of the Lamb of God that takes away the sins of the world.

Many of us are blind to sin when it is the sin of a family member or close friend. However, the words of the Lord Jesus are abundantly clear on this matter. He said in Matthew 10:37, "He who loves father or mother more than Me is not worthy of Me. And he who loves son or daughter more than Me is not worthy of Me." Are you more ready to fight for your family than you are ready to fight for Christ? Here lies one of the subtlest tricks of the devil. Many people are fooled right here. The best way to fight for your family is to be a warrior for Christ. The best way to be a bosom friend to someone is to insist that righteousness prevails. Disloyalty to Christ is the greatest threat to your family and friendships.

True believers should declare to all that no one should ask them to choose between their friendship or relationship on one hand and the Lord Jesus Christ on the other hand. It should be clear that Christ would always win. This is because Jesus is the believer's life, joy and all. It should be of none effect to be reminded by a relative of past favors, for no favor can equal the infinite payment that Christ has made for sin, and this is only the beginning of the blessings of salvation. The believer should not fear relational abandonment for the Lord had promised, "I will never leave you, nor forsake you" (Hebrews 13:5). The believer should prefer to become the black sheep of his or her family and friends than to deny Christ and prove his or her profession to be false.

LOYALTY TESTED BY THE CROWD

What happens when there is a wholesale national defection to idolatry? How should one respond when the entire group with which one identifies is committed to the wrong direction? The children of Israel were admonished to reject and banish even an entire city that embraces idolatry (Deuteronomy 13:12-18). They were to verify that such a defection is true and make sure that a 'ban' was implemented on the entire city and all of its contents. This was to be done to avert the expected judgment of God upon the entire nation.

True believers must be very careful about their associations and screen the crowd that they follow. The pressure of the crowd is very powerful. It demands conformity and threatens ostracism to the non-conformists. Here is a great test of loyalty, for everyone is tempted to be "in" with the crowd. We all want to be respected by our peers and most people around us. We are all interested in what the statistics say about what most people around us believe, think, accept or do. The people in our society with the power, notoriety, and influence are well aware of this and spend their time trying to manipulate public opinion to their advantage. They are students of the power of group dynamics. They know that the crowd can make a man put his mind, morality, and future on hold to pursue a passing lust. If enough so-called respectable people have endorsed what is obviously wrong, many people will change their views or at least reconsider their position, their better judgment.

Deuteronomy 13:14 tells us that we are to carefully investigate and scrutinize what the crowd is doing, for they are really just blindly following a few personalities with great charisma. We are not to be impressed with opinion polls for we have an infallible, inerrant, and unadulterated standard of faith and practice in the Holy Scriptures. Any city in Israel that declared independence from God in order that they might follow false gods was to be judged with utter desolation. Israel was told to execute a "ban" of complete destruction on such a renegade city or crowd. They were not to keep anything that reminded them of such wicked disloyalty before the Lord.

The seduction of the crowd partly comes from the false sense of security that it gives. The crowd tells you that so many people cannot be wrong, but you should ask the opinion of Noah when God shut the door of the Ark (Genesis 7:16). Only eight people were chosen of God for salvation in the Ark out of an entire global generation. God is obviously not impressed with popular opinion. Power does not lie in the noise of the masses, but in the still, small voice of God. The crowd gives the feeling that "we're all in this together", but the Scriptures tell us that every man shall stand individually before the judgment seat of Christ (2 Corinthians 5:10). There will be no anonymity when we stand before God. Israel was told to reject and despise the cities of apostasy. Christians are admonished to avoid the company of the ungodly and all complicity with iniquity, for the inevitable end of such is only desolation and judgment.

LOYALTY TO CHRIST

The abovementioned pressures are real and serious. The serious Christian needs to make some serious decisions if he or she is to avoid being swallowed in the disloyalty of idolatry. Here is some advice. First, the believer should maintain a holy suspicion of the spiritual advice of everyone, especially that of the obviously ungodly (1 John 4:1; Psalm 1:1-2). We should not become paranoid in our dealings with others, but neither should we forget that we are in the midst of a spiritual war. Our Christian doctrine, values, and ethical standards are not according to accepted mores and principles for living of our generation. We are fighting against the status quo. How many times have you gotten hurt because you foolishly expected or counted on the ungodly to do or say the right thing? We are better off expecting the worst from them. We can then thank God when they, even out of impure motives, are given the common grace to do the right thing to our surprise.

Second, believers should always be up front and honest about their spiritual values and distinctives (1 Peter 3:15-16; 2 Timothy 4:2). Never mislead anyone about what you really believe by beating around the bush or not telling whole truth. Full disclosure should be the Christian's policy, whether they take it or leave it. Advertise your values for all to see as well as those principles that you know are non-negotiable. This saves time, avoids temptation, prevents embarrassment and honors Christ. True believers should have no problem being fully transparent. They should have nothing to hide. Neither should they be attempting to get away with anything. Honest Christianity is always open Christianity. True believers should have no interest in blending in with ungodliness. They must be radically and explicitly different from the world. They must never apologize for their separatist position for it is a separation from worldliness, not from being involved in the world. They are being sanctified day by day in the pursuit of a greater holiness unto the Lord.

Third, believers should encourage, especially in the church, a radical obedience to the Word of God (1 Samuel 15:22-23; John 14:15; 1 John 5:2-3). This is an obedience that is built on the faith that God will never mislead His children. True believers will seem like fanatics or fundamentalist to the world because they can see that there are some issues that are not up for further debate; these are settled matters. The world looks upon such closed discussions as the result of brain washing or closed minds. The problem here is that many in the world are pretending that they have no absolutes. With clear absurdity but absolute certainty, they affirm a radical relativism with one exception: their absolute abhorrence of absolutes. God's moral law is always relevant and is never subject to the revision of opinion polls or clever debates. The Christian's test of truth is not the statistics of depraved humanity, but the infallible, inerrant Word of God (2 Timothy 3:16-17). Their responsibility is simply to obey, for the very finger of God wrote these statutes. What depraved man thinks about the Gospel is irrelevant, for it is still the power of God unto salvation to everyone that believes (Romans 1:16). What the world thinks about the Ten Commandments is irrelevant, for their value is priceless (Psalm 19:7-11) and not dependent on popular opinion.

CHAPTER 4

THE PAINFUL CONSEQUENCES OF COVETOUSNESS

M uch of the trouble in our lives has nothing to do with what someone else did to us to sabotage our progress. When the blame for our problems is being shifted around, most of it should be and will be delivered at our own front door. The monkey wrench that appears in most of our hopes and dreams often comes from our own toolbox. We are all born experts at self-destruction. This is the inheritance that we have received from the great Fall of our first parents in the Garden of Eden.

Of course, this is something that we all find very hard to admit. We prefer to blame someone else. There are therapists who are making a killing with the simple phrase "it's not your fault." We all eat it up like hot cakes. We prefer the path of evasion. Just blame it on someone else or something else. After our most corrupt, vile, and abominable indulgences, we often seek to sooth our guilty consciences by playing the "blame it" game. With this we are often very creative. If we don't blame it on our childhood or parents, we blame it on the environment or the culture. We blame it on our family, the government, our schools, the church, our diet, the television, and the list goes on and on. Though all these influences do impact our behavior, they are not the primary cause of our ungodliness. We are just like our first parents, Adam and Eve. In Genesis 3:12, Adam said to God, after he had sinned, "The woman whom You gave to be with me, she gave me of the tree, and I ate." When the Lord turned to Eve she blamed it on the serpent. Of course, none of this was, and is, and ever will be acceptable to God. We must all take responsibility for our sin.

We do not need any help in ruining our own lives. Left to ourselves, without the blessing of God's free and sovereign grace, we will at some point ignore our better judgment, gamble on our future, flirt with filth and danger, and sabotage our growth. Our problem is more than the external influences; it goes deep into the corruption of our own hearts. We do very good work when we take a man out of sin, but this is not the best work, for he is bound to return to it sooner or later. God does the best work, for he takes the sin out of the man through the blood of Jesus Christ.

How easily do we destroy ourselves! But how mightily did Jesus destroy our sin. On Calvary, "where sin abounded, grace did much more bound" (Romans 5:20). What sin erased, His blood replaced. Sordid disgrace was obliterated by Sovereign grace. Because our Redeemer died in our place, elect sinners will see the Savior's face. But apart from this grace, the prognosis of an idolatrous life is nothing but disaster.

ONE TOUCH CAN BRING RUIN

It only takes one touch, the wrong touch, to ruin your life. Be careful about what you touch. The wrong touch is the beginning of the end. The enemy of our soul does not desire any more than a touch to start the process of moral decline. He knows that the corruption within us will do the rest of this sinister work of self-destruction. He says, "Just a simple touch won't hurt...just taste and see." From the very beginning of time, the best salesmen have always given free samples, just enough to whet the appetite. We never seem to learn even after we have been burned. We buy into lines like, "If you don't like it you can always send it back." Always? Whenever we are talking about sin, we can never send it back. O how would the rich man have loved to send back his greedy days and invite poor Lazarus to his sumptuous table, but it was too late. We can't send it back. O how would Judas have loved to send back his thirty pieces of silver in exchange for peace of mind, but it was too late. We can't send it back. We all take the pretentious stance of "chalking it up to experience," but secretly we all wish we had never even touched the filth in our past to start with.

Many would love to take back that illicit sexual encounter that continues to stab the conscience. Some would love to take back those wounding words that did irreparable damage to that relationship, that act of betrayal that ruined a loved one's life, that careless attitude that wasted time and missed great opportunities, that greedy spirit that hoarded all but gained nothing or that envious heart that hated the progress of others. But while we cannot take it back, thank God, the Lord Jesus can heal it. In His hand, any stronghold of the devil can be taken back for the glory of God, any yoke of bondage can be broken, the darkest path of sin can be illuminated with the light of His grace and the worst nightmare can be turned into a dream of Beulah land. This is the promise of the Christian faith.

ONLY ONE LIE

The enemy of our souls only has one lie to tell. This lie is repeated in a variety of ways, but when you get to the bottom of it, it's the same old jingle. We have all heard the whisper in our ear, "Your case is unique; it's special. Your circumstances will excuse you. Your situation is exceptional. Hath God said...?" With every transgression, we all imagine that we can get away with it. We tell ourselves that we had no other choice. This lie of the devil is rehearsed with much variety and creativity in our minds. Do these lines sound familiar?

- "Just this once and we'll never do it again."
- "Many have done far worse than this, and they are still around."
- "We're not trying to hurt anyone; we're just trying to help ourselves."
- "We're not so bad; we really mean well deep down inside."
- "If you don't take this right now you may never get a taste of it ever again. God understands that your time is running out."
- "What's wrong with it if we are careful that no one gets hurt?"
- "Why should anyone care? We are consenting adults."
- "What they don't know about can't hurt them."

OUR IDOL OF AVARICE AFFECTS OTHERS

In Joshua 7, the invasion of the Promised Land by the Hebrew nation was in progress. Joshua, having taken the leadership after the death of Moses, had seen the mighty and conquering hand of the Lord. Israel had witnessed the tumbling down of the walls of Jericho. The Lord had given them a mighty victory by means of the trumpet, minimizing the need for the sword. It was now clearly evident that the possession of the Promised Land was not only possible; it was probable. But just when things were going fine, there was trouble in the camp. The worst is often manifested in the vicinity of the best.

God had placed a holy ban over Jericho. This meant that nothing was to be saved or salvaged from this cursed city. Nothing meant literally nothing! It meant no one, no livestock, no buildings, no personal effects and no jewels were to be spared! Nothing was to be saved or kept as spoils. Everything was to be burned in the fire of God's justice. Israel was to be a royal priesthood, sanctified unto the Lord. Nothing unclean was to be touched. The ban from God was to separate the righteous from the unrighteous. This is the essence of holiness. Separation unto the Lord is indispensable to a right relationship with God.

But all of this seemed like a total waste to a man named Achan. He figured that no one would notice if he took just a few pieces of the cursed clothing, silver and gold. He probably thought that he was not being very greedy for he was not taking as much as he could take. Achan violated the covenant. He brought the curse of Jericho into the camp of Israel. He was gambling with the future of his people. It all seemed so simple to him at first, for he didn't know that he was biting into a fruit to forfeit his future. In his greed he didn't know that he was, like Esau, selling his birthright for a bowl of potage. He didn't know that his name would forever be a gazing stock in the halls of foolishness.

Joshua knew nothing of this compromise of his spiritual defenses when it happened. He proceeded with business as usual. The next assignment was the invasion of the place called Ai on the east side of Bethel. This mission resulted in a crushing defeat for Israel. What happened? Had not the Lord promised them the victory over their enemies? Are there lessons here concerning the painful effects and consequences of our idolatry and lust on the lives of others?

THE CONFUSION CREATED BY LUST
Sin always creates confusion (Joshua 7:5-9). The children of Israel were on a winning path. They were confident that the

Lord was on their side. At this point it seemed like nothing could go wrong; they were smoothly coasting to victory. All of a sudden, like a nasty blow that came from nowhere, they suffered an awful loss. One man's sin disrupted the life of the nation. It is clear that what we do not only affects us, but those with whom we have a covenant relationship of some kind. The morale of the people melted when their pattern of victory was suddenly ended by a stunning defeat at the hands of their enemy. The Lord does not always announce His program of chastisement to His people. Sometimes He just leaves us to face the consequences of our disobedience without warning. The divine options are infinite. The Lord does not need to search long to find an instrument of correction. When there is sin in the camp, don't be surprised if your blessings are suddenly cut off, for the Lord is a holy God. When there is a compromise of His holy standards, don't be surprised if your peace and tranquility are turned into pandemonium and chaos or your laughter and joy are turned into mourning and despair. Don't be surprised if your dignity and respectability are turned into shame and disgrace and your vitality and dynamism are turned into paralysis and stagnation.

It takes very little time for sin to change the environment and atmosphere of a relationship. Intimacy thrives in holiness, but sin causes old relationships to seem like a meeting of strangers. It also builds a wall of indifference between any worshipper and the throne of Almighty God. Wherever there is confusion, there is sin. The best way to deal with the confusion is to deal with the sin. But we are often tempted to search out every other possible solution before we take the obvious one from the Scriptures. Proverbs 28:13 says, "He who covers his sins will not prosper, but whoever confesses and forsakes them will have mercy." But this doesn't seem to be enough for many people. We have convinced ourselves that our sin is not our responsibility. What God calls an abomination, we have called a disease. What God calls an offense, we have called an alternative. What God calls deviant, we have called creative. What God calls futile, we have called promising. But if we will rid ourselves of the confusion in our lives, we must abandon our sinful ways. The enemy of our souls makes a break with sin seem impossible. But if God, by His grace, has given you a hatred for your sin you can break away. It is written in Luke 1:37, "For with God nothing will be impossible." If there is confusion in your life, you don't need to pray about it for a while. You need to repent of your sin. If your life has become a tangled web, you don't need to seek professional help. The psalmist said, "My help comes from the Lord, Who made heaven and earth" (Psalm 121:2). If you can't handle the pressure any more, you don't need anyone's prayer cloth or anointing oil. You need the unction which comes from above: the anointing of the Holy Ghost. If your hands seem tied and all doors seem closed, you don't need anyone to lay hands on you. You need to hold on to the infallible Word of God. The confusion will go when the sin goes. The air will be clear when iniquity is no longer near. Deal with the sin, and God will heal you from within.

CONTAMINATION CREATED BY GREED

Sin always results in contamination (Joshua 7:10-11). We all understand the health problems that can be created with poor hygiene. It is important that we remove the germs around us, especially when we are about to eat or receive certain kinds of medical treatment. Contaminated surroundings can be fatal. With this in mind, we can also understand spiritual contamination. Holiness is the process of sanitizing your spiritual life. When God has banned something, it is only to your peril that you introduce it into your life. Death is written over everything that is cursed from heaven. In verse 11 we see a graphic description of the contamination of the congregation of Israel. The virus of greed was now invading the camp of Israel with the filth of iniquity. What began as but a small thing in Achan's house was now contagious. Its unclean effects had spread a cloud of death over the camp of Israel. This was no place for a holy God to reside. It is no wonder that the inspired psalmist asked and answered the question, "Who may ascend into the hill of the Lord? Or who may stand in His holy place? He who has clean hands and a pure heart, who has not lifted up his soul to an idol, nor sworn deceitfully" (Psalm 24:3-4).

The maintenance of a right perspective demands that we ask ourselves, from time to time, "How clean are my hands?" The faith of Abraham, Isaac, and Jacob, fulfilled in the Gospel of our Lord Jesus Christ, is the only religion that is serious about spiritual cleanliness. Some pagan religions, as well as perversions of Christianity, are proclaiming their superstitious rituals to be spiritually efficacious. Others are banking on their feeble acts of penance to compensate for mountains of guilt in sin. Others are counting on their social activism, with their pretentious concern for the welfare of humanity, to usher them into fulfillment and ultimate glory. Others are promising the gullible masses that an investment in their unique brand of religion will bring heaven on earth (health and wealth) minimizing the need for the Second Advent of our Lord in glory. But the true religion of the Holy Scriptures is not depending on the works of men, for all its hopes are wrapped up in a washing or cleansing from God. With the ever-increasing contamination in sin, we don't need another empty religious panacea. We need a good washing. When you feel the itching of sin's parasites, what you need is a good washing. You need it after rolling in the mud of perverted sensuality, especially with a mind and conscience fresh from the gutter. You need a washing, having worn garments sown in Sodom and sold in Gomorrah. You need a washing if you desire to wear God's robes of righteousness. Williams Cowper wrote in a hymn:

> There is a fountain filled with blood
> Drawn from Immanuel's veins
> And sinners plunged beneath the flood
> Lose all their guilty stains

Elisha A. Hoffman wrote in another hymn:

> Have you been to Jesus for the cleansing power?
> Are you washed in the blood of the Lamb?
> Are you fully trusting in His grace this hour?
> Are you washed in the blood of the Lamb?"

The prophet Isaiah wrote, "Come now, and let us reason together," says the Lord, "though your sins are like scarlet, they shall be as white as snow; though they are red like crimson, they shall be as wool" (Isaiah 1:18).

CONDEMNATION CREATED BY COVETOUSNESS

Sin always leads to condemnation (Joshua 7:12-13). Notice that Israel lost the favor of God in spite of their chosen status. The reason for this was that an accursed thing was in the midst of the people. God's actions will always be consistent with His holiness. There is no future in the business of sin. Any association with it will only close the door to spiritual victory. This is why it is written in Hebrews 11:24-26, "By faith Moses, when he became of age, refused to be called the son of Pharaoh's daughter, choosing rather to suffer affliction with the people of God than to enjoy the passing pleasures of sin, esteeming the reproach of Christ greater riches than the treasures in Egypt; for he looked to the reward." If you are going to stand against your enemies, you cannot walk in the counsel of the ungodly, nor stand in the way of sinners, nor sit in the seat of the scornful (Psalm 1:1). Any victory that we enjoy over the forces of evil comes from the hand of God's grace and mercy. Without His almighty hand we shall all be trampled, ground into dust, and scraped onto the rubbish heap of oblivion. Woe is the man who is left to himself, and around whom there is no hedge of divine security. To be pitied is the nation upon which 'Ichabod' has been written for a banner (1 Samuel 4:21). For when the glory of the Lord has departed all the vileness of hell is invited. It is in this environment that the dominion of sin can be expected, nothing sacred is respected, every latent vice is resurrected and all noble initiatives are thwarted.

It is a terrible thing to fall into the hands of God when He is hot with anger. When the wrath of the Almighty is kindled, do not be found in the company of iniquity. None can stand the terror of His just hand. But thank God, "where sin abounded, grace did much more abound" (Romans 5:20). Joshua 7:12 tells us that deliverance for Israel would come if the accursed thing were to be taken away from among the people. If only the cancer of Achan were removed, the salvation of Israel would be seen in the land. Condemnation in sin would then be replaced with communion with God.

When dealing with sin there can be no negotiation, accommodation, reservation and hesitation. The only way to deal with sin is to work for its destruction. Sin must be destroyed in your life. That's all there is to it. Nothing must be salvaged from sin's storehouse. The repentant sinner experiences a radical overhaul. The gambler's tables are overturned. The harlot's bed is left cold. The gossip's voice is muted. The drunkard's bottle is broken. The thief's loot is returned. Achan was removed with stones and fire. The message to Israel was clear: "...neither will I be with you anymore, unless you destroy the accursed from among you" (Joshua 7:12).

CURING COVETOUSNESS

John Piper has helped us to understand covetousness when he described it as "desiring something so much that you lose your contentment in God."[1] It is abundantly clear that when our confidence, loyalty and dependence are fully given to God, when we are fully satisfied in His sovereignty in providence, covetousness is jettisoned. Our covetousness is idolatrous "because the contentment that the heart should be getting from God, it starts to get from something else...it is a heart divided between two gods"[2]

There are some principles from the Holy Scripture that can assist in removing from our lives the covetousness that threatens to ruin us:

First, we must accept God's evaluation of whatever we desire. Consider Achan's confession in Joshua 7:20-21:

> And Achan answered Joshua and said, "Indeed I have sinned against the Lord God of Israel, and this is what I have done: 21 When I saw among the spoils a beautiful Babylonian garment, two hundred shekels of silver, and a wedge of gold weighing fifty shekels, I coveted them and took them. And there they are, hidden in the earth in the midst of my tent, with the silver under it."

It is obvious that we should never covet what God has cursed. Obedience to God's Word is a better teacher than experience. Experience, as a teacher, promises to retire your debt, but ultimately ends up increasing it. If God says something is ugly and everyone thinks otherwise, you can safely pronounce everyone to be blind. If God says it stinks, hold your nose, even if everyone else is taking a deep breath. If God says that it is dark, turn on the light of His Word, even if everyone else is sun bathing. Cherish no garments from Babylon, neither her silver nor gold.

Second, when you are tempted to sin, do not rely on personal determination; seek proper distance (1 Thessalonians 5:22). Do not rationalize—relocate! Satan's priority is to get you to hang around sin, for after this it is easy to get you hanged. Many professing Christians today are afraid of the doctrine of separation. They are trying to get as close to this world as possible and still get into heaven. Instead, their goal should be to get as close as possible to heaven even while they are still in this world. When it is really important the wise seek a responsible margin of safety. When your life depends on it, being close is not good enough; you want nothing but to hit the bull's eye. If you have been burned by sin, you will know that pretending that you can handle it is a fool's paradise. Do not be afraid to run from sin. Evasion is a powerful means of sanctification.

Third, meditate on the logical conclusion of every venture. Everything and everyone is going somewhere. Loitering is a myth. Everyone travels. The loiterer is only ignorant of his destination. Every cause has an effect. For every action there will be a reaction. "Do not be deceived, God is not mocked; for whatever a man sows, that he will also reap" (Galatians 6:7). If we would only take the time to ask about the destination of our latest fascination, we would save ourselves a lot of trouble. If God changes not, He will always hate our sin. If God is omniscient, He will always see our sin. If God is holy, He will never put up with our sin. God demands a doctrine and practice of separation from sin among His people (2 Corinthians 6:17-18).

There is an exalted position here for the true believer, but there is a condition before the position. True believers prove their position by coming out of the darkness. The call is not for ecumenism, but for separatism. The condition is that we touch not the unclean thing. James 4:8-10 says:

Draw near to God and He will draw near to you. Cleanse your hands, you sinners; and purify your hearts, you double-minded. Lament and mourn and weep! Let your laughter be turned to mourning and your joy to gloom. Humble yourselves in the sight of the Lord, and He will lift you up.

Palmer Hartsough and James H. Fillmore wrote in a great hymn:

I am resolved no longer to linger,
Charmed by the world's delight.
Things that are higher, things that are nobler,
These have allured my sight.

CHAPTER 5

CLOUDED JUDGMENT

"I told you so..." Don't you just hate to hear these words? However, the truth for most of us is that in many of our indiscretions and errors, when we honestly face ourselves, we must admit that we knew better. Then why do we do it? Why do we end up embarrassing ourselves? Why do we disappoint those we truly care about? Why do we violate the very things that we affirm we are prepared to die for? Why don't we always follow our better judgment? Don't you feel like punishing yourself sometimes?

It is clear that knowing the right thing to do, and the right reason for doing it, is not always enough to make us do the right thing. Left to ourselves we all will fall into some kind of self-destructive behavior. The apostle Paul understood this when he wrote in Romans 7:15, "For what I am doing, I do not understand. For what I will to do, that I do not practice; but what I hate, that I do." It seems as if the struggle within us to do the right thing is not as easy as it might appear. The world, the flesh, and the devil are arrayed against every one of us to encourage a spirit of rebellion against God. The world is determined to get us to conform to its corrupt values. The flesh is determined to have us compromise on God's holy precepts. And the devil is determined to get us confused concerning what is the truth that leads to life. These three enemies of our souls are focused on making rebels out of us, rebelling against our Maker.

The spirit of rebellion will make a man stupidly challenge even what is obviously invincible. Sometimes we would rather risk being destroyed than to yield one iota of our pseudo-autonomy. Our actions are clearly motivated by more than reason and common sense. The pride of man, among other things, can overrule his most prudent and sensible thought. Our culture has inflated our egos so much that most people really believe themselves to be good people without any serious character deficiency or moral pollution. They are not at all suspicious of their judgments and highly value their persons. Paul Brownback wrote:

> The greatest peril of self-love is that it is worship of self. It is idolatry with self as the idol, the antithesis of the legitimate blessedness that comes from being poor in spirit. It leads to pride toward God and selfishness.[1]

It makes no sense to tell such a man "I told you so" when things come crashing down, for he already knows what you are going to say. It seems as if we all manage to sell ourselves on the lie that our personal case is unique, exceptional, and exempt from the divinely established consequences for disobedience. Every thief believes that he is the only one that will get away with it. It just doesn't seem to matter that the statistics are not on his side. He is a gambler at heart. He believes that he can personally beat the odds. How is it that we sometimes seem so wise in our heads, but in our actions do otherwise? Just what is it that clouds our judgment?

THE WISEST FOOL

Solomon was the wisest man that ever lived. The Holy Scriptures not only tells us of how he got this wisdom from

God (1 Kings 3:3-15), but it also bares record of this inspired wisdom in the books of Ecclesiastes, Songs of Solomon, and many of the Proverbs. A powerful example of his great wisdom is the judgment he gave in a case of two women claiming the same child (1 Kings 3:16-28). He knew that the real mother would always choose to give up the child over destroying it. This wisdom brought him much wealth and political success. His fame reached all corners of the earth. His name has become a synonym of wisdom and knowledge. But there was also an amazing paradox in this man. Solomon was also one of the most foolish men that ever lived, for with such great wisdom in his head, he proved to have great folly in his heart. It makes no difference that your treasury is filled with money if you live like a pauper. This man spoke and wrote the wisdom of the ages even while he lived and pursued the ignorance of generations. It is only when precept is turned into practice that it becomes priceless.

It is important here to distinguish between a wisdom that is merely cerebral or academic on one hand, and a wisdom that is practical and spiritual on the other hand. A merely cerebral wisdom can be abused where there is no moral foundation. It may lead to an inconsistent application and used to manipulate others and situations to one's advantage. However, a truly biblical wisdom that is rooted in a character of holiness is conscientiously applied to achieve the glory of God. The former is based primarily in the head. The latter permeates the head and the heart and is expressed in the hand.

How could this wise man have such clouded judgment and be swallowed up in such folly? Are not the walls of intellectual wisdom impregnable? We all know that information is power. Those who are 'in the know' generally win, while those who are ignorant generally lose. But is there anything that can destroy those who are the most informed, even about the things of God? Just what is it that clouds a man's judgment? Is there an idolatrous link to our clouded judgment?

JUDGMENT CLOUDED BY PASSION

We are told in 1 Kings 11:1-3 of Solomon's love for the foreign women. This was in direct disobedience to the Word of the Lord. He had a massive multiplication of wives and concubines. The idolatrous pursuit of sexual fulfillment or the satisfaction of the sexual appetite has been a major factor in the demise of many a soul and the proliferation of idolatry. Coupled with this is the pride of controlling and manipulating many of the opposite sex. Solomon was the king of all Israel. His word from the throne was the civil law of the land. He had the money and power to fulfill his every fantasy. But he forgot that he was endowed by God with all of these blessings that he might be an instrument for righteousness.

In the first part of his reign we are told that Solomon loved the Lord (1 Kings 3:3). However, in 1 Kings 11 we are told that he loved many foreign, idol-worshipping women. Diplomatic marriages between the dynasties of various kingdoms were common in the ancient Near East as a means of ratifying treaties, but they were also just the pride of Oriental courts.[2] However, the multiplication of royal wives is forbidden in the law of Israel (Deuteronomy 17:17). Moreover, there were prohibitions against marrying foreign wives from the land Israel was to possess (Exodus 34:16; Deuteronomy 7:1-4; Joshua 23:12-13) because of their idolatry. But Solomon just could not have enough women. He, like many others of his generation, desecrated the sanctity of marriage, the exclusive union appointed by God at the beginning (Genesis 2:24-25). Polygamy was the accepted order of the day. No one questioned the practice for everyone who could do it did it.

The sinful heart is never satisfied with the providence of God. Even when it is obvious that there is no advantage to be gained from sexual impropriety, the depraved heart of the unregenerate man, as well as the remaining corruption of the regenerate man, invites him to indulge simply because such opportunities are available. He takes it simply because it is there. It is there to be taken so he risks everything. There is no confusion here. The immoral act is presumptuous, calculated, boastful, and daring. Every man or woman who wallows in this sinful state thinks, "Yes, I know better, but I still want it." They reason that others have done it and have apparently survived and that they can always ask for forgiveness or concoct some clever spin if there is trouble. They convince themselves that if they are careful, no one will find out, for even if others are suspicious of the sin, there will be no evidence. They buy into the lie that this will not affect anyone else. The only problem with this kind of thinking is that it fails to factor in an omniscient God. It is fallacious to the core. With every sin, we all have a clever rationalization. How easily do we convince ourselves of the appropriateness of whatever we want to do!

Solomon's polygamy was exacerbated by the fact that he was entangled with women who were committed to idolatry. He drew fire into his bosom and he got burned. When we make up our bed with sin, we will be forced to lie in it. Solomon disobeyed the call for a radical separation from the idol-worshipping nations around him. But lust will cloud the judgment of the best man around. It can become intoxicating. Self-denial, after a season of self-indulgence, seems like an elusive, unrealistic suggestion. The more you get, the more you want. This is not freedom; it is slavery to one's passions. A man is a slave to his passions when his conscience says "no" but his emotions and actions say "yes". He is hooked when he tells lies to the people he loves in order to hide the secret of his double life. He is clearly incarcerated when he is compelled to affirm the right even when he does what is wrong and when he is getting everything he wants, but is not sure that he wants what he has gotten.

JUDGMENT CLOUDED BY PERMISSIVENESS

The narrative of 1 Kings 11:4-8 makes it clear that Solomon in his old age had mellowed to the point of indifference concerning idolatry in an effort to please his idolatrous women. He not only participated in the worship of idols, but was even involved in the promotion and construction of the same.

Bad company, low morals, and old age were a volatile combination for Solomon. This combination eventually exploded into a spirit of permissiveness and chaos. We are all amused at how the older folk mellow with age. We have all watched parents who seemed to be cheap, stingy misers in young adulthood suddenly turn into generous, kid-spoiling grandparents. We have all heard and appreciated the true admonition from Ecclesiastes 12:1, "Remember now your Creator in the days of your youth, before the difficult days come, and the years draw near when you say, "I have no pleasure in them"." It is clear that old age is the worst time to find yourself figuring out what you are all about. Solomon had eaten of the fruit of wisdom, but it obviously was not digested. He had mellowed into a dangerous permissiveness. In his old age Solomon did not listen to the guidance of the prophets of God. Instead his ear was filled with the whims and fancies of his court of beautiful pagan women. His harem served him with a cup of sensuality, but he served them with his soul. G. K. Beale observed that Solomon's "great wisdom apparently did not influence his wives, but their ungodliness and idolatry influenced him."[3]

Forgetting all that his father, David, had taught him, Solomon went from bad to worse. He was so eager to please his pagan harem that he grievously displeased his Lord. Permissiveness became the order of the day. A perverted tolerance of iniquity turned into an open complicity with idolatry. The landscape of Zion was now littered with the shrines of wickedness. The anointed leader of Israel was now a follower of heathen maidens. He was led like a lamb to the slaughter by gentle body curves, smooth features, shining hair, fluttering eyelashes and soft fingers. The appointed guardian of the legacy of the chosen was now the advocate and champion of the reprobate. O how low and disgraceful we fall when blinded by the spirit of permissiveness.

It was permissiveness that took Solomon from the holy temple in Jerusalem to the abominations of paganism, from the law of the Lord to the licentious worship of the wicked and from the palace of holiness to the pigpen of emptiness. It was a perverted tolerance that took him from the fear of the Lord into the fraternity of immorality. Let us hear the admonition of the apostle Paul in 1 Corinthians 10:12: "Therefore let him who thinks he stands take heed lest he fall." How tolerant and accommodating are you of the sin and idolatry around you?

JUDGMENT CLOUDED BY PRIDE

Solomon faced divine indignation for his mutiny and repeated recalcitrance in the face of repeated warnings from the Lord. He had become bold and audacious in his idolatry (1 Kings 11:9-10). Disobedience of the precepts of God is a terrible thing. But this becomes even worst when one disobeys after one has experienced a theophany, a personal visitation from God, who came with a warning. This is true stubbornness of heart. One would think that such a personal warning from God would leave an impression on the mind and heart of Solomon, but instead he was hardened even more in his sin. It is clear that a stubborn and conceited heart cannot learn anything for it is convinced that it knows everything. Swollen heads have no advantage over empty heads. By God's grace Solomon had eaten of the fruit of wisdom.

Unfortunately, what he knew did not humble him. Pride consumed him, just like our first parents. His Adamic nature contaminated and neutralized the revelation of God that was in his mind. He suppressed the truth in pride. This suppression of truth is found in every idolater (Romans 1:21).

Before we get too impatient with Solomon, let us remind ourselves of the times when we spoke the right words, but could not hear them. How easily have we corrected others and warned them of the same dangers that have consumed us. It is so easy to give an academic endorsement of God's truth even while we have a practical contempt for it. Our stubborn and conceited hearts can rationalize a personal exemption from the path of righteousness, concocting a fallacious scenario that makes our sin appear to be an unavoidable necessity, crucial even for the pursuit of righteousness. We can all find good excuses for the worst of sins. But the real reason is a stubborn and conceited heart that must have its own way at all cost. It is rooted in our pride. But if we will not hear the voice of the Lord we are bound to feel the terror of His hand. If we will not hear the warnings of the Lord, we are bound to feel the misery of His eternal abandonment. If we will not hear the admonition of the Lord, we are bound to feel the fire of His holy indignation. If we despise the warm invitation of the Lord, we are bound to feel the cold rejection of holy justice. If we despise the soft wooing of the Spirit, we are bound to feel the hardening influence of sin. Our Caribbean forebears like to remind the young that those who will not hear, will feel!

JUDGMENT CLOUDED BY PRESENT PRIORITIES

Solomon's myopia eventually yielded some dire consequences (1 Kings 11:11-13). He failed to look down the road at the inevitable outcome of his actions. He knew enough about God that should have told him that the divine standards do not change and that our sin will find us out (Numbers

32:23) and even affect more people than we initially antici-
pated. Judgment was at his door. His nation would suffer
with division and strife. Since we are not dealing with an
ignoramus here, we can safely assume that Solomon knew at
least of the possibility of these consequences.

Solomon ignored the fact that his actions as king would
affect his whole kingdom. He foolishly ignored the fact
that God does not merely deal with us personally; He also
judges us collectively. He judges all whom we represent. We
should never imagine that our sins affect us alone. Sin not
only attacks us personally, but also our posterity. The sins of
leaders are often paid for by their followers. The sin of one
member contaminates and permeates the entire body. O how
ignorantly do we mess up the lives of others with our selfish
desires and ambition. This is irresponsibility at its worst.

It is written in Exodus 20:5-6, "For I, the Lord your God,
am a jealous God, visiting the iniquity of the fathers upon
the children to the third and fourth generations of those who
hate Me, but showing mercy to thousands, to those who
love Me and keep My commandments." What we do can
hurt those placed under our charge or those who are closely
associated with us. It is important that we are not careless
with the lives of others. Such carelessness is practically an
act of hatred and contempt. Do not be like Achan who, for
personal greed, brought the judgment of God upon the whole
camp. O that the Lord God Almighty would awaken us to the
terrible consequences of our sin. Do not be surprised if your
failure to sing God's praises causes your children to curse
His holy name. Don't be surprised if your greed and selfish
spending brings a legacy of poverty for your children. Don't
be surprised if your lack of sexual discipline is the root of
tension, chaos, and disease in your home. Don't be surprised
if your contempt for the Word of God and prayer is the foundation for rebellion and disrespect all around you. Don't be
surprised at the exposure of your irresponsibility, that you

are proven to be the main reason for the misery of others. O the destructive power of an irresponsible, shortsighted person! Such is a consequence of idolatry.

REMOVING THE CLOUD

The obvious solution is that the habits of iniquity must be replaced with the habits of righteousness. It is a process of dehabituation and re-habituation.[4] Your heart may be in the right place in terms of what you desire, but your habits are not. We are rational beings, but most of the time we do not think through things. We normally do just what we are accustomed to doing. Our habits control us most of the time. Thus, repentance must involve a radical upheaval of one's habitual life that it might be reordered to the glory of God. Everything must be examined. No stone must be left unturned. You must take a second look at those with whom you habitually converse for you will either practice murmuring or blessing. You must examine the places you habitually attend for you will either be in the company of the wicked or the wise. You must pay attention to the things that you habitually watch or read for as the saying goes, "garbage in, garbage out." You must take a second look at the teaching that you sit under, for it will either edify your mind or incarcerate your soul. You must examine the commitments of your heart, for they will either lead to irrational fear or responsible faith.

The more distrustful you are of yourself, the more trusting you will be of God (Proverbs 3:5-6). We are most vulnerable to the attacks of the enemy of our souls whenever we believe that we are invincible. The headstrong among us will soon be listed among the faint-hearted. We must be realistic and brutally honest about the corruption that remains in us. We may have been gloriously saved and delivered by the grace of God, but we are still living in sinful bodies and in a sinful environment. We have the inspired, unadulterated Word of God as our guide, but without the illumination of the

Holy Ghost we will abuse it, misinterpret it, misquote it and ignore it. The corruption that remains even after conversion is a real thing (Romans 7:18). We must take it seriously. Let us be careful not to underestimate the wickedness that we are capable of. We need to come to the rescue of those who are inexperienced in spiritual warfare. We must pray without ceasing lest we enter into temptation. It is imperative that we walk with fear and trembling, trusting God and obeying His Word, lest our judgment become or remain clouded.

CHAPTER 6

ANSWERING THE THREATS OF IDOLATRY

I n our times there are certain names that are reserved by the liberal media for people who take a strong biblical stand on matters of faith, ethics, morality, and spirituality. One of these is fundamentalist. Another name is religious right-wingers. This generation is very uncomfortable with the idea that Christians are to affirm their faith in every aspect and area of life. This scares them to death. It is not an easy thing these days to take a stand for the righteousness of God as revealed in the Holy Scriptures. We live in the so-called age of tolerance where every form of degeneracy is being given some semblance of mainstream legitimacy. If you do not join the bandwagon of the status quo that seeks to accommodate all the sinful urges and perversions, you will soon become a social outcast and will expose yourself to ostracism and ridicule. The world is clearly tolerant of everything except biblical Christianity. David F. Wells has effectively pointed out that we must define worldliness as the efforts in any culture to normalize what biblical Christianity emphatically declares to be sinful as well as when the culture conversely characterizes holiness unto the Lord as bizarre and weird behavior.[1]

As true believers in Christ, we are called not to accommodate the corruption of this age, but to expose it and destroy it through the declaration of the glorious Gospel of Jesus Christ. Yet, many who claim to be committed to Christ are wallowing in the mud of the liberal and evangelical ecumenical and inter-faith movements. Their new "gospel" is that all religions are really the same and all spiritual points of view are equally valid, so we must focus on minimizing our differences in our quest for a new unity that tolerates nothing that threatens or disturbs anyone's peace or conscience. No one must be made to feel uncomfortable. Every point of view must be respected, even if it is obvious absurdity. Because of this determination to avoid controversy of any kind as well as a zeal to promote a newly defined love which never says "no" to anything, however degenerate and abominable it may be, pressure is placed on the true believer in Christ to compromise and to never take a strong stand on anything. Thus, moral indifference and spiritual apathy are the result, and evil continues to proliferate while the true people of God stand by and do or say nothing. This is clearly a case of acquiescing to the idolatrous redefinition of our faith and our God.

A powerful example of the redefining of our faith is the contemporary church's fascination with the pop psychology that the Robert Schuller and Joel Osteen want-to-be types are proliferating in evangelical pulpits. The exposition of Holy Scripture is being displaced with therapeutic evaluations. The concept of sin has been jettisoned. It is deemed destructive to one's all important self-image. Violations of God's moral law have been relabeled as mistakes and personality flaws. David F. Wells has observed that this has produced thriving religious organizations for this new religion of Christianized psycho-babble for it "is enormously appealing to modern people who are typically preoccupied with their own inward worlds and want 'fixes.'"[2]

ACCEPTANCE AND GUILT FEELINGS

One of the main weapons of the enemy of our souls to discourage us from taking a stand for righteousness is the desire for acceptance, legitimacy, accreditation, and recognition. Satan knows that none of us want to be out on a limb all by ourselves. As social beings there is a great desire in all of our hearts to be a part of the group and to have respectable standing in the pecking order of authority. Many people just cannot stand the pressure of being in the minority, let alone standing alone on an issue. But the people of God need to remember that God is not intimidated by numbers or the absence of human recognition, for all things stand on or are disposed of according to His eternal decrees. There is a rhetorical question in Romans 8:31: "...if God be for us, who can be against us?" Believers need to do what is right and forget about what the world thinks for the highest accrediting agency is the throne of God in Glory. They may win the approval of men, but they may be wide open to the wrath of God. No man can legitimize what God calls illegitimate, but God has a cure for every form of corruption. One will never experience the peace of acceptance until one has made peace with one's Maker.

Another weapon used by the enemy of our souls to discourage us from taking a stand for righteousness is the memory of past failure. He tries to convince us that our past failures disqualify us from taking a strong stand against sin. With a clever use of irrational guilt feelings, the devil, also known as the accuser of the brethren (Revelation 12:10), seeks to nullify the effects of the substitutionary, atoning sacrifice of Christ on Calvary. By the power of the blood of Christ, true believers have been set free from their past and have been given a new beginning, but the enemy encourages them to live in fear and doubt instead of courage and faith. Believers will only take a stand for righteousness when they can forget those things that are behind them (Philippians 3:13). This does not mean that such things will never come up again. Instead, it means that whenever these things come up, they can never shut us up for our testimony is not one of earthly perfection, but of a heavenly pardon. The believer's testimony is not of personal merit, but of pure mercy. It is not one of proven fortitude, but of divine forbearance. It is not one of steadfast loyalty, but of a Savior's sacrificial love. It is not one of earning one's place, but a testimony of Sovereign grace.

When the enemy of our souls and his wicked agents remind us of who we were fraternizing with at one time, what we used to do, where we used to do it, and how many people know about it, we can just tell them that they are talking to the wrong people, for we are not our own for we have been bought with a price (1 Corinthians 6:19-20). True believers can tell them to take it up with Jesus, for in Him they have an Advocate with the Father (1 John 2:1). It is in Jesus' blood that we boast and not ourselves (Hebrews 10:16-19). The Lord has thrown all of the believer's iniquities as far as the east is from the west (Psalm 103:12). We have been asked the rhetorical question, "who shall lay anything to the charge of God's elect?" Christ has freed true believers from their past and has given them a glorious future.

THE CHALLENGE OF OFFICIAL IDOLATRY

The book of Daniel, chapter 3, tells the story of Nebuchadnezzar, king of Babylon, when he was at the pinnacle of his reign and power. He was feared throughout the world. He was ruthless, cunning, and tenacious. He did exactly as he pleased whenever he was pleased. No one questioned his authority. He was the epitome of arrogance.

The king had just constructed a massive golden statue and had decreed that all of his subjects were required to bow down before it whenever the royal orchestra began to play. Everyone obeyed except some dissidents among the king's own officials who were captives from the land of Israel. Shadrach, Meshach, and Abednego had been promoted in the royal court because of the wisdom and insight that they had demonstrated as a gift from their God. Up to this point, they had managed to keep the favor of the king without compromising their spiritual commitments. This was the greatest test of their loyalty to the God of Abraham, Isaac, and Jacob. The penalty for disobeying the king's decree was death in a fiery furnace.

Compromise was all around them. Everyone was bowing to save his or her life. These three Hebrew young men had their backs against the wall, but they did not waver in their resolve to honor their God, even to the point of death. Their political rivals in Babylon reported their disobedience to the king. Even though the counsel of these Hebrew young men was highly valued by the king, this challenge to his authority demanded a strong response of royal condemnation. It just was not politically expedient to allow such defiance to pass without the promised punishment. Such rebellion among the ranks of the royal court was scandalous. The king had to consider his options in handling this delicate situation. He angrily ordered that the rebels be brought before him that he might conduct a personal investigation of the matter.

The king's investigation was candid and concise. The choices were abundantly clear: bow or burn. Sometimes it takes an ultimatum to prove what a man or woman really believes. It's easy to take a stand and identify with the Cross of Christ when there are no threats to your life, your comforts or your conveniences. It's easy to take a stand when no one is calling your bluff. It's easy to take a stand while you are hiding in the anonymity of the crowd. It's easy to take a stand when you are involved in a religion that endorses an offering of worship to God that cost you nothing. But sooner or later, God will bring every one of us an ultimatum to prove the nature of our faith. Shadrach, Meshach, and Abednego were given the ultimatum to bow or burn. Your ultimatum might be...

- ❑ "You've got to sleep with me or else..."
- ❑ "It's either me or your church..."
- ❑ "Who cares about your day of worship, report on Sunday at 8:00 o'clock sharp or get out..."
- ❑ "If you don't cover for me, I will have to..."
- ❑ "I know what you did so many years ago, so you can't leave me..."
- ❑ "Bow or burn..."

It is clear that confronting idolatry can get dangerous. Rejecting idolatry can be very costly. The question is, will you take a stand for righteousness or will you continue to compromise? Are you prepared to trust God to work things out? Are you determined to do the right thing? Can we learn anything from the example of Shadrach, Meshach, and Abednego as they took a stand for righteousness? How did they answer the threats of this idolatrous nation and king? How can we answer the threats against us?

SETTLED ALLEGIANCE TO GOD

These Hebrew young men were clearly focused on the authority of their God over everything in life and their settled loyalty to and faith in Him (Daniel 3:16). They knew that their God was sovereign. This is what removed their worry. Charles Hodge explains it like this:

If God be a Spirit, and therefore a person, infinite, eternal, and immutable in his being and perfections, the Creator

84

and Preserver of the universe, He is of right its absolute sovereign...This sovereignty of God is the ground of
peace and confidence to all his people. They rejoice that
the Lord God omnipotent reigneth; that neither necessity,
nor chance, nor the folly of man, not the malice of Satan
controls the sequence of events and all their issues.[3]

King Nebuchadnezzar had already issued his ultimatum
with the specific challenge to their God to consider an attempt
to rescue them from his powerful hand (Daniel 3:15). These
young men responded, "O Nebuchadnezzar, we have no need
to answer you in this matter." What did they mean by this
provocative statement? Were they saying that an answer to
the most powerful political figure in the world was unnecessary? Yes! For them, this was already a settled issue. In other
words, this matter was not up for any further discussion for
no concessions could be made here. They were telling the
great king Nebuchadnezzar that he should proceed to do
what he had to do for they had done and would continue to
do what they must do. There was no question of doubt in the
minds of these men and the mortal potentate before whom
they stood that their highest allegiance was to the Potentate
in Glory who is King of kings and Lord of lords. Their allegiance was to one authority and even a discussion of defection was for them nothing but spiritual treason.

When the Lord Jesus said, "No man can serve two
masters" (Matthew 6:24) He was establishing the necessity
and inevitability of our prioritizing when we are dealing with
matters of loyalty and allegiance. This does not mean that we
are never interested in more than one thing. It means that we
cannot eat our cake and still have it. Economists may refer
to it as an opportunity cost. Every choice that we make costs
us a plethora of other options. Standing in one spot costs me
standing in another. Using my time for one thing costs me
using that same time for something else. This life is obviously

not a rehearsal. Who one proves to be now will confirm what will happen to him or her later. What we are going through now is not only real; it is really serious. Making a choice about our allegiance is not optional. A choice must be made and the cost must be counted. The God of the Holy Scriptures has a holy jealousy and He will share His glory with no one and with nothing (Exodus 20:5; 34:14). No one will ever be permitted to ride the spiritual fence with impunity. All true believers must say, like our Lord when He was tempted of the devil in the wilderness, "Away with you, Satan! For it is written, 'You shall worship the Lord your God, and Him only you shall serve.'" (Matthew 4:10).

The believer's allegiance must be to God and God alone. Of course, this is easy for one to say until one is threatened with the furnace of fire or faced with the abandonment of family and friends. It is easy to affirm this until one is actually left out in the cold. Our real character will be exposed when we must make a choice not knowing what will happen next or knowing that our resources are clearly drying up. What will we do when we can't see any light at the end of the tunnel? The three Hebrew young men spoke words that were consistent with David' words, "Yea, though I walk through the valley of the shadow of death, I will fear no evil: for You art with me; Your rod and Your staff they comfort me" (Psalm 23:4).

SETTLED CONFIDENCE IN GOD'S ABILITY

These Hebrew young men continued their testimony before Nebuchadnezzar with the words, "If that is the case, our God whom we serve is able to deliver us from the burning fiery furnace..." (Daniel 3:17a). This was no statement of doubt, but rather a testimony of confidence in their God's ability. They were able to stand up to the threats of idolatry for in the face of great danger they had some inside information, some firm theological convictions. Jehovah's power was a settled matter of faith. Nebuchadnezzar thought that he was dealing with an imaginary deity from a conquered land, but Shadrach, Meshach, and Abednego knew that they were depending on the Maker of heaven and earth. The Torah explained the ex nihilo miracle of creation wrought by the hand of God (Genesis 1:1). If God could do that, what threat is Nebuchadnezzar's fiery furnace? These young men had inside information. Believers must remember that they are dealing with a God who can calm the raging seas, turn the water into wine, heal the lame and open the eyes of the blind.

Is anything too hard for God (Genesis 18:14)? If we have any problems on this question it will undoubtedly affect our conduct. Only persons who are not yet settled on the question of God's omnipotence will feel compelled to take into their own hands matters that are rightfully divine prerogatives. Our duty involves the things which God has revealed in His Word as the means through which He will perform His eternal decrees (Deuteronomy 29:29). Our duty is to obey His commandments and precepts. We pass our place and meddle in the business of God when we are too anxious to wait on the unfolding of His secret purposes and too busy to worship Him and magnify His sovereignty in providence. The result is that we sinfully engage in manipulative devices aimed at guaranteeing certain outcomes and dreams. But this is the same thing as affirming that God lacks the ability in the circumstances of our life to work all things to the glory of His name and the good of His children. The important question here is: Do you have more confidence in your own ability than in that of the Lord God?

The apostle Paul arrived at an unwavering position on this matter. Under the inspiration of the Holy Ghost, he wrote in 2 Timothy 1:12, "For this reason I also suffer these things; nevertheless I am not ashamed, for I know whom I have believed and am persuaded that He is able to keep what I have committed to Him until that Day." Are we also persuaded? Are we convinced? Have the doubts been settled? Are we convinced that God will fight for us? Have we seen His goodness in the land of the living? Has God been faithful to His promises? We must all answer these questions, for the threats of the enemy will demand it.

CLARITY OF MIND CONCERNING GOD'S FIDELITY

Shadrach, Meshach, and Abednego knew that the God of Abraham, Isaac, and Jacob couldn't lie and that deliverance was sure to come. By faith they said, "...and He will deliver us from your hand, O king" (Daniel 3:17b). They knew that God never broke His covenant with His elect and that He never will. These Hebrew young men, who knew and worshipped the Lord in the singing of the psalms, must have, at some point, stumbled upon Psalm 118:6 in their worship and life where it is written, "The Lord is on my side; I will not fear. What can man do to me?" They knew that deliverance was sure to come. But please do not misunderstand this. They did not know how God would deliver them, but they were sure that He would for He is bound to honor His Word. They probably were not sure of the means of deliverance, but they were sure of the end. They knew that deliverance could come by death, ushering them into the presence of the Lord, or deliverance could come by some special act of providence, saving them alive. But dead or alive, their deliverance was guaranteed.

The apostle Paul, while addressing the issue of Christian forbearance and love in handling controversial matters, made an interesting statement in Romans 14:8. He wrote, "For if we live, we live to the Lord; and if we die, we die to the Lord. Therefore, whether we live or die, we are the Lord's." The apostle called upon the Roman Christians to rise above their squabbles, for in the final analysis all true believers will be safe in the bosom of the Lord.

Shadrach, Meshach, and Abednego could stay focused, even in this time of great trial, for it was clear to them that the Lord had merely created another opportunity for the manifestation of His glory. We do not have to know the "how" of God's plan before we abandon ourselves in His mighty hand. All we have to know is that the One who promises has an impeccable record and has never failed to deliver accordingly. It is written in 1 Thessalonians 5:22-24, "Abstain from every form of evil. Now may the God of peace Himself sanctify you completely; and may your whole spirit, soul, and body be preserved blameless at the coming of our Lord Jesus Christ. He who calls you is faithful, who also will do it." You don't have to know the pathway if you know the Guide. You don't have to know all the ingredients if you know the Cook. You don't need the details to exercise your faith, for faithful is He that calls you.

COURAGE ROOTED IN GOD'S WISDOM

These Hebrew young men went even further by affirming that even in the absence of an answer from their God, they would not bow to idolatry. They said in Daniel 3:18, "But if not, let it be known to you, O king, that we do not serve your gods, nor will we worship the gold image which you have set up." Now, we must make it abundantly clear that the "if" in this verse, does not question God's ability. Neither does it question the matter of whether or not God will deliver His servants. The Hebrew young men here were only entertaining the possibility that God's plan of deliverance could very well include their physical death in the fiery furnace. A sovereign God can and does include death in this plan of life. He may cause you to lose all so that you may gain everything that matters. These young men were not about to tell God how to deliver them. He could do it any way He pleased, and this did not change their loyalty. With courage they stood their ground.

We all know that our Lord Jesus let Lazarus die before He raised him from the dead (John 11:11-43). Didn't the children of Israel have to go through the wilderness before they were allowed to enter the Promised Land? Don't things often get worse before they get better? These young men were courageous, not because they were unusually strong, but because "they did not love their lives to the death" (Revelation 12:11). They did not have a death wish. They did not want to die. But they were prepared to die if they could not live to freely practice the truth. They took the position that life is not worth living if it was not lived in the will of God. They took the position of Esther who said in the face of great trial in pursuit of her spiritual duty, "...if I perish, I perish" (Esther 4:16). They took the position of Job who said of the Lord, "...even if He slays me, yet will I trust Him" (Job 13:15). They took the position of our Lord Jesus in the Garden of Gethsemane when He said in resignation and obedience to the Father, "...not my will, but your will be done" (Luke 22:42). This was not a resignation to defeat, but a cry of invincibility. Every true believer in Christ will soon learn that every set back in the life of the chosen of God is really a set up for the destruction of the works of the devil.

Such courage is rooted in the wisdom of God. It is not concerned about the outcome of things. There is a disciplined focus here on the execution of one's duty. One's eyes are fixed on the righteousness of the goal. Such courage is not interested in the score for it just doesn't matter who is ahead, for it already knows who is going to win. The true believer's eyes should not be on the score, for it should be focused on the prize. That is why we "press toward the mark for the prize of the high calling of God in Christ Jesus" (Philippians 3:14). The enemy might have a head start, but this is no problem, for his legs are bound to fail under him before we reach the finish line. The apostle John wrote, "You are of God, little children, and have overcome them: because greater is He that is in you, than he that is in the world" (1 John 4:4).

If a true believer is scared about the fact that everything is going wrong, he or she should consider Moses' dealings with Pharaoh and the Red Sea. If there is a concern about who has the largest crowd, one should have a little talk with Gideon and the reduced numbers of his forces. If there is a burden about not having sufficient resources, one should talk to Samson about the efficacy of the jawbone of a donkey in battle. If there is a concern about who has the official accreditation, there should be a conversation with Elijah about Mount Carmel and standing alone. If there is an intimidating Goliath in one's path, listen to what David said to the uncircumcised Philistine: "You come to me with a sword, with a spear, and with a javelin. But I come to you in the name of the Lord of hosts, the God of the armies of Israel, whom you have defied" (1 Samuel 17:45). God can make a way where there seems to be none.

VALIDATION AND FOUNDATION

If we no longer desire to be married to our idols and are determined to break down all altars to the same, we must seek approval only from the throne of God alone. Everyone needs affirmation of some kind. We all need to hear someone tell us that we are doing a good job. We sometimes enjoy it even when we know that it is not true. Many of us will not take a stand for righteousness because this is not what the world applauds. We must accept the teaching that a wink from Heaven is far more valuable than a standing ovation from Hell. We must stand with dignity even when the world is booing us. We must continue the work of the kingdom even when the storm of ridicule and slander are raging on every side. We must not desert our fellow soldiers in the thick of the battle. Neither must we retreat in the face of persecution and discouragement. Our Lord has admonished us in Matthew 5:10-12:

> Blessed are those who are persecuted for righteousness' sake, for theirs is the kingdom of heaven. Blessed are you when they revile and persecute you, and say all kinds of evil against you falsely for My sake. Rejoice and be exceedingly glad, for great is your reward in heaven, for so they persecuted the prophets who were before you.

Seek your approval only from the throne of God. Let His Word, His Spirit, His messengers, and His people bring you His blessings and approval.

It is also important that a believer remember his foundation, the rock from which he was hewn. This will keep him or her from being victimized by the intimidating threats of the enemy of our souls. This will help him or her to cope with the confusion of moral options. Day by day it is becoming clearer that true Christians must live as though they are constantly in enemy territory. It is becoming clearer that this world is not their home; they are just passing through. That is why we must be "...blameless and harmless, children of God without fault in the midst of a crooked and perverse generation, among whom you shine as lights in the world, holding fast the word of life, so that I may rejoice in the day of Christ that I have not run in vain or labored in vain" (Philippians 2:15-16). The Hebrew young men did not forget who they were and where they came from. They were in a strange land, but they were determined to cross over Jordan. Today, the world says, "when in Rome, do as the Romans do." But as believers in Jesus Christ, this is not our motto. We sing a different song. We will, instead, repeat Colossians 3:17: "And whatever you do in word or deed, do all in the name of the Lord Jesus, giving thanks to God the Father through Him." Shadrach, Meshach, and Abednego did not care about getting comfortable in Babylon. They had no plans to put down any roots there, for they remembered the rock from which they were hewn. That is why they must have often sung the words similar to those in Psalm 137:1, "By the rivers of Babylon, there we sat down, yea, we wept when we remembered Zion." This is the only place that we can call home. We must not forget that our goal is nothing less than repatriation in the bosom of our God.

CHAPTER 7

CONTEMPT FOR THE TRUTH

There are many aspects of our faith about which many professing Christians continue to have reservations; they find such matters to be difficult pills to swallow. They secretly wish that certain things were not in the Bible and were not required of them. They profess to be very interested in being in the family of God, but they find that they just cannot embrace the whole counsel of God. They have no strong argument against the truthfulness or the Scriptural documentation of what is required of true believers by Christ. The problem is that they prefer to pick and choose certain aspects of the faith that are most convenient and comfortable, while they reject other matters which do not promote their personal agendas. They have contempt for certain aspects of the truth.

Contempt for the truth is a very dangerous thing. It testifies of a spiritual condition which only confirms a reprobate heart if it persists. The true people of God prove their love for God by their love for His truth, even the whole truth. It is written in Psalm 97:10, "You who love the Lord, hate evil!" While the elect of God will certainly transgress from time to time the very truth of God that they love, they will be very much grieved by this, and will not manifest a consistently hardened and conceited spirit when confronted about their transgressions, but instead they will be grateful for the opportunity for repentance and the privilege of restoring fellowship that has been broken with the Lord and their Christian brethren. Even though true believers occasionally fall for the lie, they passionately love the truth and will pursue it at all costs.

The truth will be abandoned or sidelined if one is always focused on the lie. Whatever we dwell on, however ugly, will be ameliorated in our eyes if we gaze upon it long enough. Our companions do affect us. Our periodical subscriptions and book orders have a serious impact on our souls. Our mass media choices, as well as our level of intake of the same, can shape our values. Unfortunately, the influence is usually strongest in the sinister direction. G. K. Beale explains this phenomenon as it relates to idolatry with great candor:

> ...people resemble what they revere, either for ruin or restoration. God has made all people to reflect, to be imaging beings. People will always reflect something, whether it be God's character or some feature of the world. If people are committed to God, they will become like him; if they are committed to something other than God, they will become like that thing, always spiritually inanimate and empty like the lifeless and vain aspect of creation to which they have committed themselves. Such likeness to idols of the world is a form of judgment.[1]

Being seduced by the lie, with a growing contempt for the truth, is very much related to idolatry. We become more gullible when we bow to idols. Our spiritual immune system is compromised. In his discussion of 2 Corinthians 10:5, Beale comments that "Any thought that we do not bring subject to the rule of Christ is an idolatrous thought."[2] Something is clearly being valued higher than allegiance to Christ, be it an alliance, an idea, an individual or any entity.

INITIAL FIDELITY

The context of 2 Chronicles 18 presents us with Jehoshaphat, king of Judah, the southern Hebrew state, who was blessed of the Lord for his fidelity to the law of the Lord. He was God's champion against idolatry as well as a promoter of the Holy Scriptures. He hated the developments that were taking place in the northern Hebrew state, occupied by the apostate tribes of Israel which were ruled by Ahab. For this, the Lord prospered the southern kingdom of the Hebrew people. The people of Judah saw much riches and abundance. Jehoshaphat tore down the pagan shrines that were erected in honor of the heathen deities of Baal and the Ashtaroth. He made sure that his princes, as well as the Levites and priests, preached the law of the Lord continually to the people. The holiness of the Lord permeated the land to the point that all the nations around Judah feared the Lord so much that they made no war with Judah.

At the height of his prosperity, this good king fell into bad company. He sought friendship with Ahab, that wicked king of the northern, apostate tribes of Israel. This was an unholy alliance, for Ahab hated the truth of God and did all in his power to suppress it and violate it. Jehoshaphat the king, who was elevated to his esteemed position by trusting in the power of the Lord's hand, now yielded to the temptation to trust in the devices of his own hand. He sought security in compromising his principles with the ungodly and all of his progress thus far in standing up for righteousness was now in jeopardy.

UNHOLY ALLIANCES

Contempt for the truth is demonstrated when alliances are made with those who are known to hate righteousness (2

Chronicles 18:1-3). When we join ourselves to another, we marry both their merits and demerits. You cannot lie with pigs and remain untouched by the mud. The saints of God are bound to encounter the reprobate of this world, but it is not necessary for the saints to become entangled with them. Even in our closest family and business relationships, the Christian is required to declare his or her ultimate and categorical allegiance to the Christ of Scripture.

It did not take very long for Ahab, after an impressive state dinner and the related fanfare, to propose a united campaign with Jehoshaphat. The call for unity seems to be the favorite bait that is used by the ungodly to entice and entrap the godly. Unfortunately, it seems to work like a charm. But what of the rhetorical question in Amos 3:3? "Can two walk together, unless they are agreed?" The answer to this question is an emphatic "no!" We must be suspicious of all the proposals of the ungodly, even if they are relatives and acquaintances. Are we encouraging paranoia? No. We are encouraging faith in the analysis of the condition of the reprobate mind that is recorded in the Holy Scripture. It is clearly written in 1 Corinthians 2:14 that "...the natural man does not receive the things of the Spirit of God, for they are foolishness to him; nor can he know them, because they are spiritually discerned." There is a very clear call in 2 Corinthians 6:17 to "...come out from among them and be separate, says the Lord. Do not touch what is unclean, and I will receive you." The doctrine of separation is not a call to be prejudiced (in the sense of bigotry); it is a call to be pure! We are to passionately pursue holiness unto the Lord!

EMBRACING CORRUPTION

Contempt for the truth is demonstrated when there is a clear indifference to the credibility of leaders who are held up as spiritual authorities (2 Chronicles 18:4-7). In Ahab's estimation, a prophet was a prophet and a preacher was a preacher. For him, if you saw one, you had seen them all. It was no concern to him whether these men had proven that they spoke with the authority of God, being called of God. Picking the voice that you listen to is half of the fight. It makes all the difference in the world. Many people will not take the time to check out or examine the credentials, theology, morality, and consistency of the people to whom they look for spiritual advice. This is often the case when one is looking for a religious official to legitimize what is obviously illegitimate in the sight of God. The hope is that some document, some ceremony, some word of counsel, some priestly act of absolution or blessing would ease their guilty consciences and smooth over the need for real repentance and submission to the whole counsel of God in Holy Scripture. Such contempt is obvious when one celebrates only those leaders who give blind approval to sinful desires (verses 6-7). Ahab hated the prophet Micaiah, for the prophet refused to join the conspiracy of falsehood. Micaiah could not be bought. Micaiah refused to be among those leaders who were prepared to sell advice to the highest bidder. Such leaders are nothing short of spiritual prostitutes. They do not sell their bodies like the whores on the street, but they are selling their souls for the approval and honor of men and for the advancement of their personal careers in ministry. This is spiritual whoredom! God forbid that your pastor should ever tell you what you want to hear when he is certain that such counsel is a departure from the revealed will of God.

MANIPULATION BY INTIMIDATION

Contempt for the truth is demonstrated when pressure is placed upon spiritual leaders to uphold the status quo which is obviously corrupt (2 Chronicles 18:8-13). Most of us know what pressure is, especially peer pressure. When all of the respected persons in a given profession are saying one thing, it's hard to stand up and say something else. Micaiah felt the pressure that every honest preacher of the Gospel feels. The world measures credibility by the majority report. While this is certainly valuable in many cases, it cannot be the primary criterion and arbiter of truth. It is possible for the majority to be dead wrong. The final authority for all truth must be the infallible revelation of the self-contained God of Holy Scripture. He alone is the way, the truth, and the life!

The messenger that went to fetch the prophet Micaiah summarized the heart of the pressure and temptation to compromise. The messenger advised Micaiah to fall in line with the other prophets concerning how he advised the king. He said, "Now listen, the words of the prophets with one accord encourage the king. Therefore please let your word be like the word of one of them, and speak encouragement." This was the punch that was supposed to knock him out of contention. This is an example of pressure heaped on. Micaiah was being warned that not only was his message going to be negative and unpopular when others were giving a positive and enticing word, but he would have to stand alone to say it, for the opposing view had the unanimous consent of the religious intelligentsia. Talk about pressure! But Micaiah proved that he was a prophet of integrity when he announced, "As the Lord lives, whatever my God says, that I will speak."

A true servant of God cannot be bribed, for he is already rich. He is not for sale, for he has already been bought with a price. He fears no threat from man, for his life is in God's omnipotent hand. Nothing in his past worries him, for Christ has already forgiven him. He is free to declare, "Thus says the Lord," for a holy necessity is laid upon him, and divine authority stands behind him.

ARGUMENT TO THE MAN

Contempt for the truth is demonstrated when the motives of the messenger of truth are questioned in order that the truth might be evaded (2 Chronicles 18:14-17). Micaiah answered Ahab's question with sarcasm to mock the pressure tactics of Ahab's court. Of course, the king demanded that the prophet answer with seriousness. But the king's demand was pretentious for he did not want to hear the truth from the prophet. Ahab conveniently decided that the prophet Micaiah had something against him personally. This is always the retreat of those who remain conceited even when they are cornered by the truth. Instead of admitting or dealing with the truth, they prefer to contend with the messenger of truth. Instead of dealing with the issue at hand, the conceited person raises questions about the methods, mannerism, and motives of the messenger of truth. The settlement of these evasive side issues is often made a prerequisite for dealing with the real issue at hand. The hope of the conceited person is that emotional confusion will be created by such appeals, and that such emotion will grow to the point that interest in the real issue will wane. The serious Christian must ask, "How long will I allow myself to be distracted from the true issues of holiness while I bite the bait of empty, emotional side-issues?" Micaiah was not Ahab's problem. The king's problem was a stubborn, conceited heart that hated to be confronted with the truth.

MAN-CENTERED THEOLOGY

Contempt for the truth is demonstrated wherever there is an absence of knowledge of God's sovereignty (2 Chronicles 18:18-22). When your theology is basically man-centered, it is inevitable that your understanding of the world will be filled with inconsistencies. Thus, the truth of God's will and works will be very hard to swallow. Man-centered theology has no room for a divine agenda that takes priority in all things. The prophet advised these people that what happens on earth is first of all decreed in heaven. According to James O. Buswell, "...with infinite power and infinite wisdom God has, from all eternity past, decided and chosen and determined the course of all events without exception for all eternity to come."[3] The outworking of history is dependent on the internal work of the Godhead. There is a higher purpose to the events of our lives. Our plans are never the priority on this world's agenda. It is all about God and His plan. According to William G. T. Shedd, "The things decreed come to pass in time, and in successive series; but they constitute one great system which as one whole, and a unity, was comprehended in one eternal purpose of God."[4]

Ahab had a plan for glorious victory in battle, but God had a plan to use Ahab's plan to set up this wicked man for destruction. An evil spirit, like in the story of Job, was given divine authorization to use Ahab's false prophets to fool him and entice him into a conflict that would seal his doom. If you hate the truth of God, it is possible that God is setting you up for destruction. You behave the way you do because you are ignorant of the sovereignty of God in all things. You had better get used to the idea that every little thing down here is a part of something big up there. It is far better to walk with fear and trembling before the Ancient of Days.

INTOLERANCE FROM THE 'TOLERANT'

Contempt for the truth is demonstrated by the wicked when they persecute the godly because of righteous dissent (2 Chronicles 18:23-27). Micaiah was physically assaulted because Ahab's false prophet could not accept the characterization of his prophesies as being from the mouth of a demon. But the fact that truth will vindicate itself makes violence totally unnecessary. Micaiah was incarcerated for speaking up. Why were they fearful of this solitary, minority voice? It is obvious that deep down in their hearts they were shaken by the power of the truth, but the depravity of their hearts obliged them to suppress it. From the beginning of time, the voices of truth, whether crying in the wilderness and remote obscurity or stifled in the contemptuous noise of public displeasure, have always caused more disturbance than the lie. Truth cannot be ignored, even when it is whispered. People are never neutral about it. It is either passionately loved or passionately hated. If you stand for the truth you must be prepared for violent opposition. Micaiah was not worried, for the fortress of truth is invincible. The prophet knew that it was only a matter of time for the vindication of the truth. Ahab left for battle with a lie as his companion, but at the end of the battle he would lie in the bed of destruction with the truth.

ABANDONING THE IDOLATROUS LIE

There are some time-tested biblical principles with which we can navigate our way out of the idolatrous lie:

First, never apologize for carefully picking the company that you keep, for this is fundamental to guarding the truth (Psalm 1:1; 1 Corinthians 15:33). When something is put through a filter, it is refined as impurities are extracted. But when the truth is filtered through bad company, it never gets cleaner; its essence is extracted. Filtered truth is not refined; it is made filthy—a filthy lie. Hang on to the raw truth of the Word of God. It will never let you down.

Second, remember that any commitment, covenant, or agreement that is based on a violation of God's truth is not binding for the believer (Romans 3:4). You are free to abandon it. You must be loyal only to the truth of God written in the Holy Scriptures. Let no one encourage you into the irrational guilt feelings that make you feel obligated to follow through with an ungodly promise that you made. It is written in John 8:32, "And ye shall know the truth, and the truth shall make you free."

Third, waste no time in defending the tangled web of a lie, for the only way out is the truth (Acts 24:16; Proverbs 3:21-26). It is the humble way out, but it is also the only way out. You may be convinced, as you swell with pride, that you have found another way out, but you will eventually find out later that you have just gotten deeper into trouble. If God has been merciful enough to open your eyes to your folly in the season of grace, you should take advantage of God's grace and amend your ways expeditiously, for you might be blinded forever in the season of judgment.

What is your response when you come face to face with God's truth? Have you been cornered and embarrassed in the nakedness of your sin? How are you handling it? Do you look for other people to support your lie? Do you sit under leaders who will excuse your conduct? Do you pressure God's spokesmen to be silent? Do you receive godly rebuke as a personal attack? Have you forgotten that God is in control? What is your response?

We must stand up for the truth even when it is puzzling, when it is unpopular, when it is inconvenient and when it is most painful. We must stand up for the truth even when we must stand alone, when it seems like the path of failure and even when it seems out of touch, for the truth of God will stand the test of time.

CHAPTER 8

INEVITABLE JUDGMENT

It is not popular today to proclaim and teach that the God of the Holy Scriptures is not merely a God of love, but also a God of wrath. People are more comfortable with a God of mercy, but not a God of justice. However, an honest declaration of God's truth demands that both sides of the divine nature be presented, even if it makes us uncomfortable. A. W Tozer gives us an important perspective on the perils of theological shallowness when he wrote:

> What comes into our minds when we think about God is the most important thing about us. Were we able to extract from any man a complete answer to the question, "What comes into your mind when you think about God?" we might predict with certainty the spiritual future of that man....A right conception of God is basic not only to systematic theology but to practical Christian living as well. It is to worship what the foundation is to the temple; where it is inadequate or out of plumb the whole structure must sooner or later collapse. I believe there is scarcely an error in doctrine or a failure in applying Christian ethics that cannot be traced finally to imperfect and ignoble thoughts about God.[1]

The fact of the matter is that God is glorified in the manifestation of all of His holy attributes. Whenever He is pleased, all of the earth will see Him rescuing the perishing. But at the same time, at His pleasure, men will also see Him destroying the wicked. The apostle Paul wrote of our Lord in Romans 9:18, "Therefore He has mercy on whom He wills, and whom He wills He hardens." We can only beg the mercy of God for we have no right to it. He is just in doing as He pleases with the rebels in His realm.

It is interesting to see how men can get proud and presumptuous concerning their positions and stations in this life. In many instances, they have either bought into the idea of an impotent God or the idea of an absent God. Basically, they see themselves as both the playwright and the actors in the drama of life. They really believe that they call the shots. They laugh at any talk of a sovereign God, for they see no restraints on their wicked devices and actions. They see no impediments to their decadent, perverted hedonism. Their bellies are full as they eat with gluttony from the table of vice that is spread before them daily. Their schemes seem fool proof. The clever lining of each pocket seals the lips of all who could blow their cover. They ask, "What could possibly go wrong?" As far as they are concerned, they have been getting away with the wickedness for so long that there must be something wrong with God. They reason that if God is good, then he must be weak. They also reason that if God is strong, then he must not be good. So, with this false sense of security created by their apparent "success" at evil, they eat, they drink, and they are merry, reasoning that if the wickedness has not caught up with them by now, it probably never will. But C. S. Lewis reminds us that the justice of God is a matter that demands long-term evaluation, for we may view it in this life as incomplete or imperfect, but in the broad scope of eternity God's justice will be complete.[2]

The Holy Scriptures tells us that the wicked shall have a rude awakening if the Lord is pleased to leave them in their darkness. The psalmist David wrote that "The wicked plots against the just, and gnashes at him with his teeth. The Lord laughs at him, for He sees that his day is coming" (Psalm 37:12-13). So let the wicked have his laugh now, for we know who will have the last laugh for his day is coming. Amidst the call for justice in the land, the just are victimized because they lack the right connections, even as they watch the wicked conveniently pulling the strings of nepotism. However, the righteous should never lose heart concerning this for it is promised that the wicked man's day is coming. Our contemporary society is celebrating all kinds of immorality with an open castigation of biblical morality. Trusting souls on every level are being deceived, but it is promised that very soon the wicked man's day is coming.

We shouldn't worry about losing a battle if we know that we will win the war. We shouldn't mind putting our corn in the ground when we know that we will reap an abundant harvest in due time. The holiness of the just will yield the happiness of heaven, but the happiness of the wicked will only yield the horrors of hell. The psalmist David confirms this with the words, "A little that a righteous man has is better than the riches of many wicked. For the arms of the wicked shall be broken, but the Lord upholds the righteous" (Psalm 37:16-17). The same God who will show his mercy will also show His justice.

JUDGMENT ANNOUNCED

The prophet Amos announced to the ancient Hebrews of the northern kingdom of Israel that the judgment of God was imminent on what he called the 'day of the Lord' (Amos 5:18-27). In the midst of all of their material prosperity during the reign of Jeroboam II, this idolatrous nation had forsaken the commandments of the Lord. The outward prosperity had exposed their inward corruption. They had removed all authority and sought to make subjective judgments on all moral and spiritual matters as if the Lord had not spoken. They found convenient justifications for all of their evil. They even managed to keep up a lot of religion and ceremony through which they attempted to legitimize their illegitimacy. But every generation of man, in all of the evil and depravity, soon learns that God is a just Lord. There is a time when judgment is sure. There are some important lessons from Amos' announcement of judgment. What was the condition of these people that opened them to the wrath and terror of the Lord God Almighty?

WAITING IN VAIN

A false sense of security is an awful thing. It is a terrible thing because you are assaulted when your guard is down, when you are basking in a fraudulent safety. The prophet Amos announced the word of the Lord saying,

> Woe to you who desire the day of the Lord! For what good is the day of the Lord to you? It will be darkness, and not light. It will be as though a man fled from a lion, and a bear met him! Or as though he went into the house, leaned his hand on the wall, and a serpent bit him! Is not the day of the Lord darkness, and not light? Is it not very dark, with no brightness in it? (Amos 5:18-20).

What kind of people is he talking to? These are the people who make life one big gamble. They keep their fingers crossed, knock on wood, and hope for the best. They do not make their calling and election sure. They live as they please with the gamble that in the end there will be a special dispensation from God that absolves them of all evil and wipes their evil slate clean. Such is the wishful thinking of fools.

This is like the picture of the man who is late for work every day, and who maliciously misses work on many days, but who is present and early on payday. He is waiting in vain if he is hoping for full wages.

Some people are actually expecting our Lord, at the time of judgment, to ignore what they have asked for all of their lives. But our God is a just Lord. He doesn't tamper with the mail. At the time of judgment he will deliver to you just what you ordered. If, in your sin, you hated the light and loved the darkness, in judgment God will simply say, "You may have it." If in arrogance you despised God's way and sought your own way or in your quest for happiness you went after that which is sensual and sinful instead of that which is spiritual and saving, God may just let you have it. With intellectual pride you received only that which was clever and evasive instead of that which is truthful and redemptive, so in judgment God may simply grant you your position. In judgment God simply delivers what we have been requesting for the entirety of our lives.

There are very few things that are worse than a false sense of security. It is very important that one is sure that he or she is not waiting in vain. We must be very careful. Assuming that things are fine does not make them fine. Salvation is not in some religious group, church ceremony, charitable act, or a good reputation. Salvation is of the Lord. The evidence of this salvation is true repentance and faith, followed by the public testimony of believer's baptism and a life of loving obedience to God's precepts. Let everyone give diligence to self examination. The apostle John wrote in 1 John 2:28, "And now, little children, abide in Him, that when He appears, we may have confidence and not be ashamed before Him at His coming. If you know that He is righteous, you know that everyone who practices righteousness is born of Him." Our only security is abiding in the Lord, not in some man-centered scheme. With the latter you will merely run from the lion to meet the bear. Sin makes you take refuge, not in a house of rest, but a serpent's pit. There is no light, but perpetual darkness. God forbid that you are waiting in vain.

WORSHIPPING IN VAIN

Even though worship might appear to be quite orthodox and biblical with the external forms, it could still come up to the true and living God as an exercise in idolatry. The prophet Amos continued to speak for the Lord with the words:

> I hate, I despise your feast days, and I do not savor your sacred assemblies. Though you offer Me burnt offerings and your grain offerings, I will not accept them, nor will I regard your fattened peace offerings. Take away from Me the noise of your songs, for I will not hear the melody of your stringed instruments. But let justice run down like water, and righteousness like a mighty stream (Amos 5:21-24).

This describes the person who is foolish enough to believe that the Lord is easily impressed with either his solemn or ecstatic religious acts. The fact of the matter is that the Lord is impressed only with holiness, justice, and righteousness. Whether it is medieval asceticism or contemporary, charismatic ecstasy, empty religious displays will not serve to impress God or mitigate one's position before God's throne of judgment. All of our vain religious ceremonies, shallow songs, grudging offerings, and empty promises will be received with nothing but contempt from God if His grace is not manifested in our lives.

If our worship is not based on God's work of grace in our lives, we are wasting time. We are all tempted to appeal to our family tradition and legacy in a particular religious group as evidence of a solid foundation that we feel compelled to perpetuate. But this is never the issue with God. If our act of worship is more important than the object of worship (which should be Jehovah alone), such worship is vain, hypocritical, empty, and a waste of time. Even if it is colorful, interesting and entertaining, true worship demands that God is given His worth.

There are many religious groups that should be abandoned immediately if one cares about one's soul, for such entities care nothing about the proclamation and encouragement of holiness. The psalmist David wrote, "Give unto the Lord the glory due to His name; worship the Lord in the beauty of holiness" (Psalm 29:2). When you give God your time in worship, it means nothing if His grace has not changed your cold, stony heart giving you the warmth of a heart of flesh. When you give God your talents and abilities in service for the kingdom, it means nothing if you are not motivated by His love in your heart. When you give God your tithes and offerings, it means nothing if you have not sacrificed every-thing on His altar. He demands that "justice run down like water, and righteousness like a mighty stream."

You may recite as many prayers as you want. You may demand that every solemn, religious ceremony be admin-istered to you. But all is vain if the Spirit of God has not given you true repentance and faith. The true people of God, according to John 4:24, worship Him "in spirit and in truth." Be careful that you are not worshipping in vain.

WORKING IN VAIN

Whenever there is an important investment of one's resources, it is crucial that one ascertain some idea of the efficacy of one's efforts. The prophet Amos continued the admonition from God with the words,

"Did you offer Me sacrifices and offerings in the wilderness forty years, O house of Israel? You also carried Sikkuth your king and Chiun, your idols, the star of your gods, which you made for yourselves. Therefore I will send you into captivity beyond Damascus," says the Lord, whose name is the God of hosts (Amos 5: 25-27).

Idolatry is hard work. This would be just fine if the key to success in life was merely hard work. But it is not merely hard work that yields success in life. The nature of the work itself is far more important than the intensity of one's exertions. Idolatry is hard work because it is a substitute for the real thing. What a foolish and futile work it is for a man to attempt to give a job, an idea, a possession, or a person the stature and importance of the person of the Lord God Almighty. But man has been attempting this from the beginning of time. C. J. H. Wright explains that "the primal problem with idolatry is that it blurs the distinction between the Creator God and the creation. This both damages creation (including ourselves) and diminishes the glory of the Creator."[3] The idolater is not just redesigning his concept of God; he is also addressing his concept of self. Every man has a passion or obsession. We need to make sure that our passion and our obsession are found in loving and serving the Lord, or we are merely working in vain.

Many have used their busyness as a cover for their secret rebellion. They would rather not deal with the deeper issues of the faith, so they crowd their lives with all kinds of activity, even religious activity. But note well that all of such activities do not necessarily serve the Lord. Often, such activities only serve their selfish appetites. The vast majority of mankind, even the religious, is pouring more of its energy into temporal things than in spiritual and eternal things. Is it not because they are earthly-minded? The apostle Paul wrote in Colossians 3:2, "Set your mind on things above, not on things on the earth." Some professing Christians are actually disturbed or disgusted when they are challenged to invest in eternal things. The work of the Gospel ministry is a burden to them. It is getting in the way of their so-called important business, which often turns out to be more the nursing of their greed than the meeting of their true needs.

What is the nature of your work? What is your passion? Where do your affections lie? Wherever there is the work of idolatry, you can be sure that exile, alienation, and destruction are right around the corner. There is no doubt that you are working in vain.

YOUR VIEW OF GOD

Avoiding the wrath of God requires a change in one's view of God. There must be a mental revision of one's theology that also warms one's affections and activates one's will. The mushy, impotent, one-sided god, which many imagine, is not the God of the Holy Scriptures. This invention is merely the product of man-centered religion and a vain imagination. The God of glory is indeed loving and merciful, but only His people, the elect of every nation, will share these eternal blessings. However, let there be no confusion on this point. He is also a God of wrath and justice. He will execute His vengeance upon all who live a life that mocks His holy name. Every soul needs to demonstrate that God has given them the grace to flee their sin and the wrath to come. Have you been waiting in vain? Have you been worshipping in vain? Have you been working in vain? Your only hope is to cry out to God for mercy and "let justice run down like water, and righteousness like a mighty stream."

CHAPTER 9

RELIGIOUS REFORMATION

M any people are disgusted by the proliferation of religious groups in the world today. A plethora of sects
have emerged on the scene as people experiment with all
sorts of mystical and speculative ideas in their quest for a
meaningful life. The failure of some of the extreme cults has
not cooled the general public's interest in religion, even in
its most eccentric expressions. Both deep interest and tired
disgust are juxtaposed in the public's response to the developments in religion. On one hand the interest grows because
our sophistication and educational advances have not given
us the fulfillment that such had promised. Contemporary
society is disappointed concerning the scandalous emptiness
that remains in the hearts of the most 'successful' of men
and women, who drive the news headlines with their many
creative means of self-destruction. The more people seem to
achieve, the unhappier they seem to become. Many of these
disillusioned people are now looking again at religion as a
possible solution to the emptiness.

On the other hand, others have grown more cynical and
skeptical as they resist the idea of a religious panacea. They
are just disgusted by what they perceive to be a conspiracy
of deceit in religion. They have judged that the world has

enough problems, so additional religious complications are not welcomed. There is even the suspicion that religion is at the heart of the world's problems, and there is ample historical data of religious intrusion into the various problems in the world to give credibility to such a suspicion. The concerns raised are issues that cannot be ignored by the true churches of Jesus Christ that derive their faith and practice from the Holy Scriptures.

Many people are concerned about the confusion that is created by this growing religious phenomenon. Just which one is right? Upon what authority or evidence do the different groups make their claims? On a more practical level, many people are troubled about the use of religion by many to enrich themselves at the expense of those who are at a vulnerable stage in their lives. It is obvious that people who are in deep poverty or debt, as well as those who are emotionally and relationally in distress, are easy prey for the religious con artist. The secular con artist is obviously an immoral person, but a religious con artist seems to scrape the bottom of the pit of human depravity.

Are we witnessing a new trend or is it not just the recurrence of the age-old contest between truth and falsehood? Should we panic as we watch the current affairs in religion? Has not the truth always stood alone in the midst of a multitude of lies? Has the naked truth ever really panicked upon the approach of the most sophisticated lie? Has not the truth always held its ground, being vindicated by the test of time? Is there any doubt that the truth will endure? Has it not made its way through the congestion of error in generations past? And will not this generation pass as well?

We should never worry about how many have joined the contest, for the place of victory is an exclusive and solitary place. In the final analysis, only the truth will be left standing. So let all the religions of the world show their face, both the old and the new. Let them present their case, for truth is a thing that does not need to boast or win popular appeal. All who do not stand with her in the day of reckoning will fall before her in defeat and banishment. Biblical Christians, the true believers in Jesus Christ, are not shaken by the trends, for it is their conviction that the ultimate triumph of the truth will not be merely the celebration of a concept or philosophy, but more so the exaltation of a Person: Jesus of Nazareth. It was Jesus who said, "I am the way, the truth, and the life. No one comes to the Father except through Me" (John 14:6). Our problem is not with religion, but with false religion. Did not James speak of a religion that is pure and undefiled (James 1:27)? True religion has not died, for the Spirit of Truth still reigns supreme. The question before us is: What reforms are essential for the flourishing of true religion?

ESTABLISHED FALSE RELIGION

In 1 Kings 18, the prophet Elijah sought such a reformation of religion in Israel. Ahab, the apostate king of Israel, and his notoriously wicked queen, Jezebel, had promoted the false religion of Baalism in the land. The sacrilegious shrines of Baal poisoned the landscape of Israel. To this, God responded by permitting a famine and drought to overtake the land. The spiritual wasteland had resulted in a physical wasteland. It is obvious that we must never forget that all things are related to spiritual things. The king and queen had done much to promote Baalism, even to the extent of killing the prophets of the Lord, and most of them hid and ran for their lives. It was truly a dark day in Israel.

The prophet Elijah and the king could not fellowship together. How could they? "Can two walk together, unless they are agreed?" (Amos 3:3). Elijah himself had been a fugitive for some time. But the time had come for a showdown. There is a time in all our lives when all of the running must stop. We must then turn around and face our problems head on. This is the time to stop the posturing and take direct, positive action. This is the time to test the veracity of all claims. Elijah announced to the servant of the king that he was prepared to have a face-to-face meeting with the monarch. When Ahab met with Elijah they both accused each other of being the "troubler of Israel." Well, it was clear that all of the confusion was somebody's fault. Elijah was determined to get to the bottom of this. He did not ask for a blue ribbon committee or a royal commission of inquiry to investigate the matter. Neither did he request an independent counsel or an ombudsman. He proposed a challenge for a meeting of the prophets of Baal and the prophet of the Lord Jehovah on Mount Carmel to prove which religion served the real God.

The showdown on Mount Carmel was set up. At first it seemed a bit lopsided. There were 450 prophets of Baal standing against one prophet of Jehovah in a place that had the favorite shine of the Baal worshippers. Baalism had the numbers as well as what seemed to be the home court advantage. True believers should never panic at whatever is arrayed against them on this earth, for the battle is not theirs but the Lord's (2 Chronicles 20:15). Elijah was sure to fail if it was a battle between men, but his victory was imminent for Jehovah's name is El Shaddai, the Lord God Almighty. Elijah then challenged the 450 prophets of Baal to prepare a sacrifice. They were to call Baal to ignite the fire, since they claimed that he was the god of the storm and fire or lightning. Elijah would do the same thing and call upon the Lord. It was agreed that the deity who answered from heaven with fire was the true and only God who alone should be served.

The Baalites prepared their sacrifice and began a daylong ritual designed to evoke Baal's response. Doing a sort of limping dance, they circled the altar, crying, "O Baal, hear us!" Noon came, but there was no response from Baal. 1 Kings 18:26 says, "But there was no voice; no one answered. Then they leaped about the altar which they had made." Elijah then made some mocking, sarcastic remarks and suggested that they were not crying loud enough; that Baal was meditating, relieving himself, traveling, or perhaps just sleeping. The frenzy among the Baalites increased. They were becoming desperate, for their emptiness was about to be exposed. They cut themselves with knives, hoping that the flowing of blood would invoke a response. But according to 1 Kings 18:29, "there was no voice; no one answered, no one paid attention."

When evening came, the exhausted Baalites gave up their futile efforts. Elijah went into action! It was time to begin the process of reform. This was the moment that he was waiting for. God had cornered the enemy of our souls. Just what did Elijah do? What steps are necessary for reformation in the face of false religion?

REBUILD THE INFRASTRUCTURE—
THE ALTAR OF GOD

In war, no army can win without the necessary infrastructure. This infrastructure is more than up-to-date weaponry. It also includes secure communication lines, support facilities, warning systems, and so on. It just doesn't matter how trained your soldiers are, without the necessary infrastructure defeat is inevitable. Effective education also needs infrastructure. Without the necessary apparatus or means to record, retrieve, and communicate information, educational initiatives and institutions are doomed to fail. Every community or village needs good infrastructure if it is to function smoothly. To prevent turmoil, basic facilities, services, and installations, such as transportation and communications systems, water and power lines, roads and bridges, and public institutions including schools, post offices, and prisons must be established and adequately maintained. A proper infrastructure is indispensable to any institution or cause.

The prophet Elijah knew that the first thing on the agenda had to be the rebuilding of the infrastructure of true religion (1 Kings 18:30-35). The altar of communion with the true God had to be restored. We are going nowhere spiritually until the altar of the Lord is rebuilt. Until there is once again a place in our lives that forces us to look up to the Almighty, instead of deifying our lusts and greed, we shall remain trapped in the abomination of idolatry. We are actually controlled by what we worship. What we worship brings us into intimate contact with and under the powerful influence of the object of worship, whether that object is Christ or demons.[1] The enemy of our souls knows that if godly institutions are preserved by a return of the focus on the true and living God, holiness will flourish. This is why Satan is determined to pervert the home and subvert the church. This is why he is determined to sabotage the assembly of the saints as well as your family and personal devotional times. This is why he is determined to make your Bible gather dust on some shelf. This is why he will encourage you to steal the tithe that belongs to the Lord. This is why Jezebel had broken down the altars that were built to the glory of Jehovah. Elijah knew that the rebuilding of the altar had to be his first initiative if reformation was to come.

When the altar is rebuilt with stones that represent the chosen people of God, the people are reminded of whom they are, from whence they have come, and the filth in which they stand. Why should the seed of Israel, the one who wrestled with God, be subject to the agents and idols of the heathen? Why should the living stones of Christ be heaped among the tombstones of iniquity? O what shame and mockery overtake the chosen of God when they forget the foundations upon which they were built. The saints of God must make the restoration of such an altar in the name of the Lord the priority of their lives. They must publish anew the Gospel of sovereign grace, and rid the pulpits of the pop psychology of our generation. They must sing God's praises in the profound verse of Scripture, not the "cross-over" seduction of the contemporary lyric. They must catechize the young with sound doctrine, lest the minds of this generation are stolen with idleness and perversion. They must lift the banner of holiness, and turn back the tide of secularism and lawlessness in the land.

The prophet Elijah was not satisfied to merely rebuild an altar as a monument to the presence of Jehovah. His altar would also magnify the power of the Almighty. The altars of idolatry were built as monuments to the presence of false gods, but this testimony was betrayed by the absence of fire upon their sacrifices. The prophet Elijah mocked the impotence of their false gods by increasing the margin of difficulty. He ordered that the altar be drenched with an abundance of water. Igniting such an altar would be more difficult. He would make it abundantly clear that the God of Abraham, Isaac, and Jacob did not depend on trickery or the manipulative devices of men. El Shaddai is all-sufficient in His power and might.

In like manner, true believers are challenged to drench God's altar with the water of their troubles, but God is yet able to do the impossible. They may cover His altar in an avalanche of their sin, and He will melt it with the warmth of His grace. They may immerse His altar in the confusion of their hearts, but the light of His fire can illuminate the path to Glory. They may saturate His altar with the burdens of their past, but He will lighten their load by igniting a glorious future. Is anything too hard for God? Behold the glory of God's omnipotent hand! God's glory shall be evident in all the land. So, go ahead and wet down His altar for our God is a consuming fire and He delights in doing the impossible.

RE-INTRODUCE THE GOD WHO IS SOVEREIGN

The form of worship reflects the object of worship. How you worship testifies of what or whom you worship. The worship of false gods neither has the simplicity nor the depth of the worship of Jehovah. False worship is focused upon that which pleases men and is indifferent to that which is an abomination to God. False worship emphasizes sensationalism for it has no substance. False worship is obsessed with ritual for it is not based on reality. False worship is entangled with the politics of the day for it is not grounded in divine prophecy. False worship boasts in the statistics of its followers and finances for it knows nothing of the power of integrity. False worship emphasizes empty liturgical forms while it ignores profound theological foundations. False worship has no passion for purity for it is not based on a godly morality. False worship is on a quest to impress, manipulate and appease a god, but true worship approaches God in spirit and in truth (John 4:24). What is the nature of your worship?

The prophet Elijah knew that the sovereignty of God must be the focus of attention in true worship if there is to be real reform (1 Kings 18:36-39). He did not waste any time with vain repetitions for the God of Abraham, Isaac, and Jacob was neither deaf nor indifferent. The prophet simply and humbly called upon the Lord to verify His identity, vindicate His servant, and validate His Word. He said,

And it came to pass, at the time of the offering of the evening sacrifice, that Elijah the prophet came near and said, "Lord God of Abraham, Isaac, and Israel, let it be known this day that You are God in Israel and I am Your servant, and that I have done all these things at Your word" (1 Kings 18:36).

This is the heart of true worship. Everybody needs to know just who He is, just who represents Him, and just what He has said. The prophet then called upon the Lord to act so that all glory might be ascribed to His matchless name for the turning of the hearts of the people (verse 37).

The Lord answered the prophet's prayer with fire from heaven. The Lord will always respond when true worship that magnifies His sovereignty is restored. The Divine response was not based on a formula or format of prayer. The response came because the prayer of faith had tapped into the flow of the Divine purpose. It is not our prayers that change things; it is only the immutable will of God that changes things. Efficacious prayer is that which is rooted in the revealed will of God. The blessings of God are not arbitrarily bestowed. Only petitions that are immersed in and conformed to the Divine revelation are honored with fire from on high. Such prayer is worship par excellence, for it offers to the Ancient of Days only what He has required. When prayers like this go up, it doesn't take long for the fire from heaven to come down. Every saint should pray that the fire of God would come down in like manner upon our apostate land. They should petition the Lord that the purifying flame consume the dross of our sin and bring conviction to the sinner. We need a fire from heaven today. The fire came down to expose the falsehood, and affirm the truth. It came down to erase all confusion about just who has the rightful claim to the kingdom, the power and the glory. The fire came down that righteousness should prevail in all the land. It came to mock the efforts of the wicked, and mark the beginning of their end; and to exalt God's humble servant, in whom He was well pleased. Fire came down when true worship went up, to the glory of the Father. It took the fire from on high to bring these wayward people to their knees. It took direct Divine intervention to break up the fallow ground and remove the stony hearts. It took a display of Sovereign power to bring about submission and an admission that "the Lord, He is God!"

REMOVE THAT WHICH THREATENS YOUR RELATIONSHIP WITH GOD

The prophet Elijah ordered the execution of the perverted prophets of the false god according to the laws that God had given Israel (1 Kings 18:40; Deuteronomy 13:5; 18:20). This is because the holy and the profane have no common ground. In the contest between truth and falsehood there is never a stalemate. One will be left standing and the other will fall. Reformation will never come until we are determined to purge our ranks of everything that manifests an allegiance to false religion. This is often a painful and difficult undertaking, but nonetheless necessary. Such a stand for righteousness is often subjected to charges of an absence of compassion, a spirit of arrogance, a dance of hypocrisy and an encouragement of an unforgiving spirit. But we should ignore such charges for it is never unloving to destroy ungodliness. This is a noble, biblical end. However, the means that we use should always be remedial and gracious. The best way for us to destroy the wicked is to pray for his transformation. Evil is destroyed by the triumph of good. But the God of Abraham, Isaac, and Jacob, who doeth all things well, is sometimes glorified, not in the granting of pardons, but in the ordering of punishments. God has other ways and means for destroying evil, and Elijah used that which was legitimate according to the law of the land. God's arm of justice was swift and sure. Holiness unto the Lord often demands spiritual surgery. The strongholds of the enemy had to be destroyed.

Reformation never comes with merely defensive warfare. The soldiers of the Cross of Christ must take up offensive positions to corner the enemy or force him into retreat. It is written in James 4:7, "Therefore submit to God. Resist the devil and he will flee from you." There is a place for dialogue, but it should never displace the necessity of discipline. There is a place for admonition, but it should never eliminate excommunication. There is a place for compassion for sinners, but it should never degenerate into complicity with sin. There is a place for embracing the broken of heart, but we should be careful not to reward the unrepentant. There is a time to wait for God to expose those who are corrupt, but there is also a time to hunt them down and smoke them out of their hiding places and "let not one of them escape."

The prophets of Baal had become entrenched in Israel. They were the religious and political elite with the backing of the monarchy. As long as they remained in positions of respect and veneration, Israel was bound to remain under the domination of iniquity and idolatry. They had to be removed and destroyed. The prophet Elijah knew that having exposed the hypocrisy of idolatry, he had to finish the job. His mission was more that winning an argument or debate about theology; his goal was to crush the enemy of true religion. It is only with a zero tolerance of evil that sufficient discipline is maintained for progress in righteousness. A zeal for the eradication of evil might seem a bit idealistic, but it is a mark of a well-grounded believer.

Of course, this is not an Islamic jihad type of call to commit genocide against unbelievers. Our times are different and our means are not violent (Romans 12:21), but we must be just as clear in our opposition to and mobilization against falsehood and evil. Many may think that you are over-reacting in your fight against the wickedness around you, but wisdom demands a margin of safety between you and the evil. Do not be discouraged. Go ahead and finish the job like David and cut off Goliath's head, for the Lord's anointed should never bow to an uncircumcised Philistine. Finish the job and burn the cities of Moab and Edom, for the incarceration of evil begins the emancipation of good. Finish the job like the saints who marched until the walls of Jericho tumbled down, for the elect will not take possession until the reprobate face eviction. Finish the job and break down the thrones and scepters of paganism around you, for the temple of the Lord is for those with clean hands and pure hearts. Like Elijah, finish the job and slay the perverted advocates of Baalism who threaten the progress of true religion.

DELIBERATE AND CAREFUL ACTION

We must be careful to guard against the practice of presenting facts without the truth. This is how the most effective lies are concocted. Facts must be interpreted. Truth and falsehood are both interpretations of the same facts. Our analysis must be mature. We must not be gullible and assume that the presence of a few facts means that we are even in the vicinity of the truth. It is possible that the agents and spokesmen of false religion may wax eloquent on issues of morality and ethics even while they subvert the foundations of the faith. False religion may also be housed in the centers dedicated in the name of the true and living God. Let us never grow complacent concerning this. False religion has subtly woven itself into the fabric of life. You may have been victimized already without knowing it. But you will know it when the light of God's Word shines upon it (2 Timothy 3:16-17). You will never see it without such light. The illuminating power of the Holy Ghost locates, penetrates, exposes, and disposes of all that is void of the pure truth of God. Without the Word and the Spirit we are gullible, vulnerable, and doomed to fall for the lies of false religion.

It is also important that we do not envy the sensual worship of others, for worship is not for our pleasure, but God's. No one had a better show than the prophets of Baal, but the efficacy is not in the 'Showtime' religion; the power is still in the old-time religion. True and biblical spiritual leaders have given up on competing with popular religion.

They realize that they cannot win the statistical game played by those who imagine that one's ministry is validated by crowds, finances and theatrics. Eugene Peterson described the challenge of the true prophets of God in the face of Baal worship.

> Baal religion is about what makes you feel good. Baal worship is a total immersion in what I can get out of it. And of course, it was incredibly successful. The Baal priest could gather crowds that outnumbered the followers of Yahweh 20 to 1. There was sex, there was excitement, there was music, there was ecstasy, there was dance....And what did the Hebrews have to offer in response? The Word.[2]

When the true saints of God are gathered to worship Him, their offering might seem a bit simple. Their songs might lack worldly sophistication. Their houses of worship might seem a bit plain and without elaborate ornamentation. Their messages might at times ignore the accepted conventions of rhetoric and oratory. Their order of worship might not include pageantry, processions and mystical rituals. But if it pleases God, who cares about societal expectations or demands? If it is a sweet smelling savor around the throne of heaven, who cares? If it is blessed with a harvest of sin-sick souls, who cares? If the presence of the Lord is felt in the midst of it, who cares? If it is answered with fire from on high, who cares?

True believers should not be afraid of the contest between righteousness and wickedness for the true and living God can take care of Himself. They should not panic even when everything crumbles around them or murmur at the profanity and cursing around them for God knows the end from the beginning (Isaiah 46:10). They should not retreat even with the casualties and losses around them or lose hope even when falsehood has taken the strategic mountain on the battlefield. They should hold out for reform and never settle for less.

CHAPTER 10

PASSING THE TORCH

How long does it take to dismantle everything good that has been built up in our lifetime? How long does it take for all the values that we hold dear to disappear from the land? How long does it take for the doctrines that we love, believe, and teach to appear as strange and foreign teachings in the land? How many generations does it take for us to move from Christian holiness to pagan heathenism? How fast can the slide be from theism to atheism and from true religion to idolatry? There is a case to be made that demolition is far easier than construction.

History has already shown us that it only takes one generation to repudiate and dismantle the achievements that were built by many generations that precede it. How easily does today's generation spit on that for which our forefathers gave their blood. With no sense of history or with an arrogant exaltation of the present, many people today tear down fences without ever stopping to ask why these fences were built. Many are disillusioned for they have no use for precedent in making their decisions since they possess only a cursory knowledge of where they came from. As a result they do not know where they are supposed to go, and they end up improvising and using guesswork with the important issues of their lives and the lives of others. This is a formula for nothing but disaster.

ABORTED MISSION

In Judges 2, the children of Israel upon invading the Promised Land of Canaan had made a great error. God had placed a curse or ban on the inhabitants of the land. He therefore ordered His invading people under Joshua to expel the cursed and idolatrous Canaanites from the land. These people were to be completely destroyed as well as all that they possessed. The only reward that one can get for mingling with a cursed or banned people is to share in the curse and the wrath of God that would fall upon these people. The children of Israel chose instead to make alliances with the cursed people. They clearly believed in a multiculturalism that made all religious positions equally valid. Thus, truth was a relative matter to them and the truth of God was marginalized. Many were enticed into the false fertility cults of the land and many intermarried with the Canaanites. One verse in the book of Judges puts the state of affairs in a nutshell. Judges 17:6 says, "In those days there was no king in Israel; everyone did what was right in his own eyes." Were not these people, the chosen of God, to be a light to the nations? How could they survive and maintain their distinctives with such wholesale assimilation into idolatry? What factors led to the spiritual decline of that generation? Are there lessons here for our generation?

TRANSFERRING THE LEGACY OF FAITH

The Hebrew people got distracted from their mission and failed to transfer the legacy of faith (Judges 2:7-10). A whole generation rose up who did not know their roots, why they came to that land, and what standards God had prescribed for them. There was a difference between Joshua's generation and the one that followed it. Something significant died with Joshua. The spiritual inheritance was not transferred. It only takes one generation for a people to move from biblical theism to abject paganism.

It is becoming increasingly difficult to convince the so-called spiritual people in today's churches that spiritual concerns should be paramount in their lives. Everyone seems to be so busy at this business of making a living and on 'getting ahead' that matters like devotion to God and being grounded in the faith are being sacrificed on the altar of personal greed and ambition. The new gospel which proclaims the right to good health and much wealth has eclipsed the message of holiness unto the Lord in many instances. Our young people are being spoiled by the ease with which they always get what they want, but not necessarily what they need. We are producing a generation that is nothing but fruit that is harvested too early, a generation that considers it a right to have adult experiences and information while they are yet children without any regard for the spiritual context or consequences of such experiences. So the youth are allowed to go anywhere, watch any show, wear anything, hang out with anyone, speak in any manner, and study anything without being responsible or accountable to anyone. We are producing a generation that values nothing spiritual and embraces hedonism as its primary motivation. The tail is wagging the dog and the cart is pulling the horse. We need to return to the biblical priority of biblical parenting or we will continue to witness the decline of a generation and national ruin.

Our young people are being spoiled by parental tolerance of the slow-kill, poisonous influences of the culture. They are being spoiled by parental apathy towards the ministry of the church and Christian education. They are being spoiled by parental neglect of discipline and training, by the parents' readiness to interpret their children's rude behavior as childhood creativity. They are being spoiled by parental inconsistency and immorality, for their parents' lack moral authority owing to parental immorality and unethical behavior. Is anyone in charge of the homes in the land? There has been a coup d'état in most homes. The children seem to be in charge. Parental abdication of responsibility is clearly one of the most serious problems of our generation. The so-called experts on relationships, the secular priests with their degrees in psychology and sociology, have so carefully labeled every problem with technical and esoteric jargon that even people in the churches are impressed with the terminology and actually believe that these people have answers that are not in the Word of God or answers that are superior. Thus, many in the churches are walking in the counsel of the ungodly, standing in the way of sinners, and sitting in the seat of the scornful (Psalm 1:1).

It's high time that parents stop tiptoeing around their children's temper tantrums and show them who really should be in charge. We need some tough love in our families. It's high time that parents quit asking for their children's opinions about what is obviously right or wrong and start demanding their compliance with the Word of God. We need parents who will stop bowing to the pressure of the popular culture and start promoting the righteousness of God without fear or compromise. It's high time that parents stop listening to the unholy therapists of idolatry and start listening to the Holy Spirit of God as He illuminates the Holy Scriptures. We need parents who will stop living for their personal lust and start living for the glory of God and the good of their children, transferring the legacy of faith once delivered to the saints.

IDOLATROUS LIFESTYLES FLOURISHING

Are idolatrous lifestyles flourishing unabated? Is what is happening today anything like what was happening in Judges 2:11-13? The generation that came after Joshua was not engaged in nominal or tagalong idolatry. They became champions of idolatry. They didn't just admire the mud; they were rolling in the mud. Baal and Ashtaroth were fertility idols, so the worship services always were lustful displays that ended in sexual orgies. We are witnessing a similar phenomenon today. The children of many reputedly godly parents, who were considered pillars of the community, mock the memory of their parents with the stench of their degenerate lifestyles. Such a generation is not content to merely question the righteous views of our forefathers. They feel compelled to confront, condemn, and contemptuously contend with righteousness. Thus, their intoxication surpasses the most notorious drunkards, their laziness and treachery exceeds the worst of the vagabonds, their profanity surpasses the foulest of mouths, their revelry overshadows the worst orgy, and their values make sewage look like drinking water. They let themselves go. Anything goes.

Behind every season of spiritual and moral decline is a sacrifice to a false god. Like the generation that came after Joshua, we are witnessing the proliferation of shrines erected to contemporary idols of health, wealth and self-esteem. Holiness is not passionately pursued by most. The worship of God has been displaced as the top priority with the pursuit of power, pleasure, property, popularity and financial prosperity. And these days the money seems to come less and less from the factory of honest labour and more and more from the laundered, ill-gotten gain. But this is not the worst part. The most frightening development is that the churches are dragging these idols before their worshippers. The only difference is that such idols have been renamed with theological and religious terminology and whitewashed with biblical quotations. This assimilation of paganism into the church has come upon us like an avalanche. It is so powerful that holiness is no longer in the mainstream. To be separated from worldliness and reserved for righteousness is a dangerous thing these days. Ostracism, ridicule, victimization and marginalization describe the plight of those who remain faithful to Christ.

Most people are no longer satisfied with the churches that preach holiness without compromise, for there are a plethora of religious alternatives that promote happiness without conscience. Seminaries and Bible Colleges now train church leaders in the art of entertaining the people with the so-called relevant strategies for marketing the message. They have little use for bold proclamation that exposes sin, demands repentance and faith, and promotes obedience to the revealed statutes of God. There is greater focus upon the style of worship rather than the substance of worship as religious groups compete with one another by giving the people what they want.

All principles of morality are under attack. The churches that are afraid to offend the hedonistic addictions of the people ignore the profaning and abuse of the Lord's Day. There is a growing anti-authority attitude in our generation with a deep resentment for structure and discipline, and the churches have become a part of the problem as church officials, for fear of their ecclesiastical competition, refuse to take a strong stand on any issue. The churches are mute about the wanton slaughter of unborn babies every week, all for the convenience of the sexually promiscuous in its ranks. Unrepentant whoremongers are not disciplined in the churches for today's call for tolerance and compassion does not include hating sin. The impenitent extortionists and gamblers are not rebuked at church if they remember to give a generous offering or fraction of their plunder. An extreme subjectivism is promoted so that truth can never be narrowly defined and is never absolute. Thus, lies are given more credibility and more publicity than the truth. Religion is now openly used as the tool of the greedy as they covetously plunder the needy. These are but a few examples of the fact that the lifestyles of idolatry have flourished unabated.

COUNTING THE COST OF SIN

The legal penalty of sin was collectively applied to the Hebrew nation as they suffered the consequences of sin (Judges 2:14-15). They were exposed to the exploitation and plunder of their enemies without divine protection. This divine response was necessary and inevitable. God's holiness demanded this. Some have suggested that the holiness of God is the most important single attribute of God.[1] A holy God, by definition and according to His nature, must eventually move to destroy sin. If judgment seems long in coming, do not imagine for a moment that there is a lack of resolve in the One who sits on the throne of Glory. He only seems to tarry because He is very patient in waiting for His appointments. But He always keeps His appointments.

Always remember that sin has both personal and corporate consequences. Our sins will most certainly affect our own lives as well as the lives of those with whom we fellowship. God indicts us both as individuals and as a people. The corruption of sin permeates one life and contaminates other lives. The wrath of God, in cases like this, is multiplied to the point that the only appropriate divine response to this corporate culpability is a mass outpouring of terror and abandonment.

Why are we so surprised at the wrath of God? The Lord Jesus clearly had as much to say about it as He did about the subject of the love of God. There is no mystery here. A holy God must condemn that which is unholy. It is only in the grace, love, mercy, and forbearance of God that we find mystery. The fact that God can pull the latter off can be called nothing less than amazing. Only God could do that. Wrath is the appropriate divine response to our sin.

God poured out His wrath against Israel by removing the hedge of protection that He had placed around them (verse 14). He didn't have to slap them; He merely let them go. He simply exposed them to the enemy of their souls. He left them naked and vulnerable. Whenever we are tempted to question whether God is doing anything for us, we must remember that He is always holding up the fence of protection. Sometimes that looks like inactivity, but you only see its importance when you are exposed to the enemy of your soul.

It is crucial that we take note of the fact that the wrath of God was in accordance with His warnings and threats. Judges 2:16 explains that he called out judges to warn the people. God finds no sadistic enjoyment in the outpouring of His wrath. The satisfaction of justice is a necessary element of holiness. We must always remember that powerful reminders of God's consistency always precede the wrath of God. This is what a warning is all about! God must deliver whatever He has promised, even when the promise is wrath in response to our disobedience. Lest we are consumed in the wrath of God, our generation needs to address the fickleness and infidelity that poisons all relationships, the rudeness and disrespect that sabotages all learning, the apathy and laziness that hinders all our labor, and the depravity and hardness of heart that cancels all hope.

FEARING MAN RATHER THAN GOD

We can be sure that we are not responsibly passing the torch of righteousness to the next generation when we see the hardening of the hearts of our youth against the things of God. This is being done in the face of the obvious lovingkindness and mercy of God. This mirrors the experience of ancient Israel (Judges 2:16-19). Judges were appointed to warn them. They ignored the warnings. Then the judges delivered them anyway. But when the judges died, they simply returned to their idolatry. They possessed hardened hearts.

The wisdom of God always finds a way to demonstrate His covenant love even while He demonstrates His faithfulness to justice. Even when God had turned the spoiler loose, He had also appointed a deliverer! God is a God of mercy. He does require punishment, but, thank God, He also rescues the perishing. He does pass by some that justice may be satisfied, but, thank God, He calls out some who, through His blood, are justified. Even after God had provided a judge to deliver His people, they initially refused to listen to the Word of the Lord. In His mercy, God brought relief and deliverance anyway. But the people only responded positively as long as a judge was alive. They became even more corrupt when a judge was not around to watch them.

We are witnessing the demise of a generation when people respond favorably to men even while they maintain their contempt for God. A stubborn and stiff-necked people not only have a hard time listening to and receiving the truth about themselves, but they will eventually begin to play religious games with God. If you must be watched before you will do what is right then you have not done anything from the heart and it matters nothing. If your obedience must be monitored, you must count yourself among the chief of hypocrites. If you are motivated only by careful surveillance, then you must be advised that you are concerned about the wrong eyes; you are yet to understand the sovereignty and omniscience of God.

DIVINE COUNSEL VERSUS HUMAN ANALYSIS

It is only natural for there to be some cry for deliverance when evil is obviously entrenched around us. However, there are certain circumstances under which such cries are heard but are also ignored by God. Lingering instability is one of God's ways of purging a people. Where there is a state of normalcy and the status quo is being reinforced, no one pays attention. Thus, instability and destabilization become important tools in the divine plan. This is the state of affairs where there is no rest in the land. At one moment there is some semblance of peace. Then, suddenly, there is a volcanic eruption of violence. At one moment there is some semblance of uprightness, but it is short-lived for it was but a charade in a carnal scheme of corruption. The only thing that is consistent is the moral and spiritual inconsistency. There is a perpetual spiritual seasickness as men and women are rocked to and fro on the waves of iniquity broken by brief moments of calm. This is a generation that is in a constant state of flux. The effects of instability linger on and on.

Our generation has striking parallels with ancient Israel in which there was the lingering effects of instability (Judges 2:20-23). God had promised that there would be no comprehensive deliverance of the children of Israel from their enemies in Canaan as a consequence for their sin. God would sometimes use the lingering persecution by the enemy to chastise those who were truly His and expose those who were not. Even today we also dwell in the midst of a people of unclean lips. Idolatry is entrenched all around us. The enemy of our souls is well financed and fortified around us. There is no doubt that there always comes a time when we all get tired of the status quo. We are ready for a revolution. We have prayed for change, but it seems like our cries for divine intervention are all rejected at heaven's gate. This is indicative of a generation in decline.

The enemy will not go away for the wheels of divine justice are already rolling, and separation will take place only at the time of harvest. The enemy will continue to persecute for the laws of reciprocity must take their course: what you sow you will reap (Galatians 6:7). There will be instability until the hand of Lord renders Satan impotent and until the Lord comes and takes His people away (John 14:1-3).

HOPE FOR OUR CHILDREN

Are we to resign ourselves to the demise of the next generation? God forbid. We are to learn from the experience of ancient Israel and work for the systematic indoctrination of our youth in the fundamental doctrines of the faith (1Timothy 4:2). This is spiritual warfare. We are fighting for their souls. We have no time or use for competing ideologies that are foreign to the Holy Scriptures, for what can any man say to improve on the holy, inspired, inerrant, infallible, and unadulterated Word of Almighty God? Our youth will have a fighting chance in engaging the ideologies of idolatry, whether philosophical or animistic, if they are grounded in the doctrines of the faith. We must not apologize for this indoctrination, for idolatrous atheism catechizes and indoctrinates the youth of our generation in its poisonous doctrines, such as evolution, without any shame or embarrassment over a charge of indoctrination.

There is also a need for aggressive evangelism with the message of God's free and sovereign grace (Ephesians 2:8-9). All men everywhere must be told that salvation is of the Lord, for there is no other Gospel. The problem of sin is far too serious for a man-centered solution. It takes nothing less and nothing more than the unconditional election of God the Father, the definite atonement of the God the Son, and the effectual and efficacious calling of the Holy Ghost and the preserving grace of God enabling a man to persevere in righteousness. All of the above is indispensable in saving a man from his total depravity and inability in sin. All other man-centered schemes at salvation will succeed only in temporally perpetuating the idolatry of man and eternally landing men's souls in an eternal Hell. It literally took a divine rescue mission to accomplish every sinner's salvation. Salvation is of the Lord.

A plan for saving our generation cannot be complete without affirming holiness as the primary evidence for assurance of salvation (Hebrew 12:14). We must show very little patience for those who would invent other priorities for the Christian life, priorities such as ecstatic and bizarre utterances and experiences, mystical rituals and ceremonies, materialistic acquisitions, hedonistic pursuits, or idolization of the Jewish Sabbath with other forms of Reconstructionist legalism. If our Christianity does not result in making us holy onto the Lord, with nothing less than an ever-increasing separation from worldliness and sin, it is bogus, empty, fallacious, futile, and a waste of our time. If we will save a generation we must be holy.

Let us refuse to give up on our children. It is obvious that judgment is at the door, but there is room at the cross for all of the chosen of God. As long as we are alive, we must believe that there is hope. As long as God is on the throne, we must believe that we can cope. As long as someone will listen, we must stand in the gap with the truth. As long as God continues to open doors, we must enter into service with boldness. As long as there is a remnant according to God's grace, we must offer up praise and thanks to the Author and Finisher of our faith.

NOTES

INTRODUCTION
1. B. S. Rosner, "Idolatry," in *New Dictionary of Biblical Theology*, ed. T. D. Alexander and B. S. Rosner (Downers Grove, Ill.: InterVarsity Press, 2000), p. 571.
2. Tim Keller, "Talking About Idolatry in a Postmodern Age," April 2007, http://www.monergism.com/postmodernidols.html
3. John Piper, *Future Grace* (Sisters, Oregon: Multnomah Publishers, 1995), p. 9.

CHAPTER 1—THE TEMPTATION OF THE DANCE
1. G. K. Beale, *We Become What We Worship: A Biblical Theology of Idolatry* (Downers Grove, Ill.: InterVarsity Press, 2008), p.84.
2. J. B. Phillips, *Your God Is Too Small* (New York: Macmillan, 1961) pp. 63-66.
3. *The Wycliffe Bible Commentary*, edited by Charles F. Pfeiffer and Everett F. Harrison (Chicago: Moody Press, 1962), p. 82.
4. Tom Steller, "Little Children, Keep Yourselves From Idols," June 1985, http://www.desiringgod. org/ResourceLibrary/Sermons/ByDate/1985/495_ Little_Children_Keep_Yourselves_from_Idols/

CHAPTER 2—THE DISPLACEMENT OF GOD

1. Richard Gaffin, "Speech and the Image of God," in *The Pattern of Sound Doctrine: Systematic Theology at the Westminster Seminaries*, Essays in Honor of Robert B. Strimple (2004), p. 186.

2. F. Samuel Janzow, *Luther's Large Catechism: A Contemporary Translation with Study Questions* (St. Louis: Concordia Publishing House, 1978), p. 13.

3. J. I. Packer, *Concise Theology: A Guide to Historic Christian Beliefs* (Wheaton, Il: Tyndale House Publishers, Inc., 1993), pp. 26-27.

4. John Calvin, *Institutes of the Christian Religion*, ed. John T. McNeill; trans. Ford Lewis Battles; Library of Christian Classics, XX-XXI (Philadelphia: Westminster John Knox, 1960), Book I. Ch. 4. Section 1.

CHAPTER 3—THE DISLOYALTY OF IDOLATRY

1. Augustus H. Strong, *Systematic Theology* (Westwood: NJ: Revell, 1970), pp. 567-573.

CHAPTER 4—THE PAINFUL CONSEQUENCES OF COVETOUSNESS

1. John Piper, *Future Grace*, p. 221.

2. Ibid., p. 221.

CHAPTER 5—CLOUDED JUDGMENT

1. Paul Brownback, *The Danger of Self-Love* (Chicago: Moody Press, 1982), p.130.

2. *The Wycliffe Bible Commentary*, edited by Charles F. Pfeiffer and Everett F. Harrison (Chicago: Moody Press, 1962), p. 322.

3. G. K. Beale, *We Become What We Worship: A Biblical Theology of Idolatry*, p. 306.

4. Jay E. Adams, *The Christian Counselor's Manual: The Practice of Nouthetic Counseling* (Grand Rapids: Ministry Resources Library, Zondervan Publishing House, 1973), pp. 180-190.

CHAPTER 6—ANSWERING THE THREATS OF IDOLATRY
1. David F. Wells, *God in the Wasteland* (Grand Rapids: Eerdmans, 1995), p.59.
2. David F. Wells, *Losing Our Virtue* (Grand Rapids: Eerdmans, 1998), p.203.
3. Charles Hodge, *Systematic Theology* (Grand Rapids: Wm. B. Eerdmans Publishing Co., 1952) vol. 1, pp. 440-441.

CHAPTER 7—CONTEMPT FOR THE TRUTH
1. G. K. Beale, *We Become What We Worship: A Biblical Theology of Idolatry*, p.284.
2. Ibid., p. 305.
3. James Oliver Buswell, *A Systematic Theology of the Christian Religion* (Grand Rapids: Zondervon Publishing House, 1978) vol. 1, p. 163.
4. William G. T. Shedd, *Dogmatic Theology* (Grand Rapids: Zondervan Publishing House, 1971 reprint), vol. 1, p. 395.

CHAPTER 8—INEVITABLE JUDGMENT
1. A. W. Tozer, *The Knowledge of the Holy* [New York: Harper & Row, 1975], pp. 9-10.
2. C. S. Lewis, *The Problem of Pain* (New York: Macmillan, 1962), pp. 144-154.
3. C. J. H. Wright, *The Mission of God* (Downers Grove, Ill.: InterVarsity Press, 2006), pp. 187-88.

CHAPTER 9—RELIGIOUS REFORMATION

1. Charles Hodge, *Commentary on the first Epistle to the Corinthians* (Grand Rapids: Eerdmans, 1965), pp. 194-195.
2. Eugene Peterson, "Spirituality for All the Wrong Reasons," *Christianity Today*, March 2005, p. 45.

CHAPTER 10—PASSING THE TORCH

1. Augustus H. Strong, *Systematic Theology*, p. 297.